SOCIAL ISSUES
FIRSTHAND

Street and Runaway Teens

Other Books in the Social Issues Firsthand Series:

Street and Runaway Teens

Cynthia A. Bily, Book Editor

GREENHAVEN PRESS

An imprint of Thomson Gale, a part of The Thomson Corporation

Detroit • New York • San Francisco • New Haven, Conn. • Waterville, Maine • London

THOMSON

GALE

Christine Nasso, *Publisher*
Elizabeth Des Chenes, *Managing Editor*

© 2008 The Gale Group.

For more information, contact:
Greenhaven Press
27500 Drake Rd.
Farmington Hills, MI 48331-3535
Or you can visit our Internet site at http://www.gale.com

LIBRARY OF CONGRESS CATALOGING-IN-PUBLICATION DATA

Street and runaway teens / Cynthia A. Bily, book editor.
   p. cm. -- (Social issues firsthand)
Includes bibliographical references and index.
ISBN-13: 978-0-7377-4033-2 (hardcover)
1. Homeless youth--United States. 2. Runaway teenagers--United States. 3. Homeless youth--Services for--United States. 4. Runaway teenagers--Services for--United States. I. Bily, Cynthia A.
  HV1431.S83 2008
  362.74--dc22

                2007036126

ISBN-10: 0-7377-4033-7 (hardcover)

Printed in the United States of America
10 9 8 7 6 5 4 3 2 1

Contents

Chapter 3: Trying to Help Teens in Trouble

Foreword

Social issues are often viewed in abstract terms. Pressing challenges such as poverty, homelessness, and addiction are viewed as problems to be defined and solved. Politicians, social scientists, and other experts engage in debates about the extent of the problems, their causes, and how best to remedy them. Often overlooked in these discussions is the human dimension of the issue. Behind every policy debate over poverty, homelessness, and substance abuse, for example, are real people struggling to make ends meet, to survive life on the streets, and to overcome addiction to drugs and alcohol. Their stories are ubiquitous and compelling. They are the stories of everyday people—perhaps your own family members or friends—and yet they rarely influence the debates taking place in state capitols, the national Congress, or the courts.

The disparity between the public debate and private experience of social issues is well illustrated by looking at the topic of poverty. Each year the U.S. Census Bureau establishes a poverty threshold. A household with an income below the threshold is defined as poor, while a household with an income above the threshold is considered able to live on a basic subsistence level. For example, in 2003 a family of two was considered poor if its income was less than $12,015; a family of four was defined as poor if its income was less than $18,810. Based on this system, the bureau estimates that 35.9 million Americans (12.5 percent of the population) lived below the poverty line in 2003, including 12.9 million children below the age of eighteen.

Commentators disagree about what these statistics mean. Social activists insist that the huge number of officially poor Americans translates into human suffering. Even many families that have incomes above the threshold, they maintain, are likely to be struggling to get by. Other commentators insist that the statistics exaggerate the problem of poverty in the United States. Compared to people in developing countries, they point out, most so-called poor families have a high quality of life. As stated by journalist Fidelis Iyebote, "Cars are owned by 70 percent of 'poor' households. . . . Color televisions belong to 97 percent of the 'poor' [and] videocassette recorders belong to nearly 75 percent. . . . Sixty-four percent have microwave ovens, half own a stereo system, and over a quarter possess an automatic dishwasher."

However, this debate over the poverty threshold and what it means is likely irrelevant to a person living in poverty. Simply put, poor people do not need the government to tell them whether they are poor. They can see it in the stack of bills they cannot pay. They are aware of it when they are forced to choose between paying rent or buying food for their children. They become painfully conscious of it when they lose their homes and are forced to live in their cars or on the streets. Indeed, the written stories of poor people define the meaning of poverty more vividly than a government bureaucracy could ever hope to. Narratives composed by the poor describe losing jobs due to injury or mental illness, depict horrific tales of childhood abuse and spousal violence, recount the loss of friends and family members. They evoke the slipping away of social supports and government assistance, the descent into substance abuse and addiction, the harsh realities of life on the streets. These are the perspectives on poverty that are too often omitted from discussions over the extent of the problem and how to solve it.

Greenhaven Press's Social Issues Firsthand series provides a forum for the often-overlooked human perspectives on society's most divisive topics of debate. Each volume focuses on one social issue and presents a collection of ten to sixteen narratives by those who have had personal involvement with the topic. Extra care has been taken to include a diverse range of perspectives. For example, in the volume on adoption, readers will find the stories of birth parents who have made an adoption plan, adoptive parents, and adoptees themselves. After exposure to these varied points of view, the reader will have a clearer understanding that adoption is an intense, emotional experience full of joyous highs and painful lows for all concerned.

The debate surrounding embryonic stem cell research illustrates the moral and ethical pressure that the public brings to bear on the scientific community. However, while nonexperts often criticize scientists for not considering the potential negative impact of their work, ironically the public's reaction against such discoveries can produce harmful results as well. For example, although the outcry against embryonic stem cell research in the United States has resulted in fewer embryos being destroyed, those with Parkinson's, such as actor Michael J. Fox, have argued that prohibiting the development of new stem cell lines ultimately will prevent a timely cure for the disease that is killing Fox and thousands of others.

Each book in the series contains several features that enhance its usefulness, including an in-depth introduction, an annotated table of contents, bibliographies for further research, a list of organizations to contact, and a thorough index. These elements—combined with the poignant voices of people touched by tragedy and triumph—make the Social Issues Firsthand series a valuable resource for research on today's topics of political discussion.

Introduction

Although estimates vary, each year approximately 1.5 million young people in the United States—more than half of them between the ages of 15 and 17—leave home suddenly under difficult circumstances. Some run away, while others are sent away by parents or guardians. Covenant House, an organization that serves and shelters troubled teens, describes its clientele this way: "In most states, a runaway is anyone under 18 who leaves their home (or other residence) for one or more nights without the permission of his or her parents (or legal guardians). A homeless teenager is anyone under 18 who has no home to return to and needs supervision and care. Throwaways or lockouts are kids who have been thrown out by parents or guardians, feel unwelcome at home, or that there is no place for them in the family. When we talk about homeless and runaway youth, we talk about these young people too." Many runaways find that while they may have gotten away from adults at home who seemed unable or unwilling to protect and care for them, the adults they find on the streets are no more nurturing. Each year, some five thousand young people on the streets die of suicide, illness, drug abuse or violence, and thousands are forced by adults to work as prostitutes or drug runners.

Until the 1970s local, state, and federal governments tended to punish rather than to help young people in trouble. Teens who ran away from home were often treated as criminals. It was illegal for minors to run away from home, no matter what their home situation was like, and runaway teens who were caught were arrested, and were likely to be found guilty of "status offenses" (acts that are crimes only because of the young age of the perpetrator) and either placed in juvenile detention facilities or returned to troubled homes. Although many local communities attempted to help young people in trouble, teens knew that asking for help increased their chances of being arrested or sent back home. In 1974 Congress adopted a new attitude and passed the Juvenile Justice and Delinquency Prevention Act, which provided financial assistance for states to operate programs for street and runaway teens, as well as guidance for those programs. In return for the money, states eliminated criminal penalties for running away.

One of the programs funded by the federal government is the National Clearinghouse on Families and Youth (NCFY), a program of the U.S. Department of Health and Human Services. Rather than see street and runaway teens as criminals, the NCFY understands that "young people need support, guidance, and opportunities during adolescence, a time of rapid growth and change. With support, they can develop self-assurance in four areas key to a happy, healthy, and successful life: a sense of competence, a sense of usefulness, a sense of belonging, and a sense of power." Many young people who find their way to support programs and shelters have access to alternative schools, job training, counseling, and other services that can help them stay safe and work toward promising futures, even if they are never able to return home.

In addition to new attitudes about runaway teens, the Internet has opened up new possibilities for teens and their families to get help. A simple Google search for "runaway teens" turns up almost a million hits, alongside dozens of ads for organizations offering aid. For decades, organizations like the National Runaway Switchboard (NRS) have provided 24-hour-a-day toll-free hotlines. Posters in bus stations and other public places have urged young people to "Call 1-800-RUNAWAY if you are a teenager who is thinking of running from home, if you have a friend who has run and is looking for help, or if you are a runaway ready to go home." With the Internet available even to displaced teens through public libraries, cell phones and other devices, the NRS has expanded its services to include a bulletin board "where you can post your questions, thoughts, and concerns about what it feels like to be a teenager or a parent. If there's something you've been wondering about, please ask. Chances are good that a lot of other people have been wondering the same thing." Covenant House, which has operated its Nineline hotline (1-800-999-9999) for decades, has also developed an online presence, so that teens can send e-mail or post messages.

Parents, too, have turned to the Internet, combing through the bulletin boards of NRS, Covenant House and other groups looking for news of their missing children. Web sites have been set up specifically to offer advice and emotional counseling for parents. Team HOPE, for example, is staffed by volunteers who describe themselves as "ordinary people, who one day were forced to live every parent's nightmare. We know the pain, the fear, the frustration and the aloneness of having a missing child."

Another group with an important Internet presence is the National Center for Missing and Exploited Children. NCMEC maintains an online CyberTipline, a Web site where anyone may file a report of suspected "cases of child sexual exploitation including child pornography, online enticement of children for sex acts, molestation of children outside the family, sex tourism of children, child victims of prostitution, and unsolicited obscene material sent to a child." The CyberTipline, which has processed almost half a million reports since its founding in 1998, forwards information to the appropriate law enforcement authorities. Ironically, the Internet can be a tool to help and to hurt troubled teens. In one NCMEC "success story," a 17-year-old girl ran away from home "to live with an adult male she met on the Internet." Stories like this, involving young people who are lured from home by people they meet online, are increasingly common. However, adults working to protect teens are also computer savvy, including the NCMEC analyst who located the missing girl in Florida by examining the girl's networking website for clues, and then searching the Web for information that led police to the home where she was staying.

Because there are so many young people in trouble, and because many of the groups working to help them are large and operate anonymously, it can happen that the statistics seem to overwhelm the individual people concerned. In *Social Issues Firsthand: Street and Runaway Teens*, the authors, including teens themselves, parents and other family members, and people who have worked in various programs to help troubled youth, remind readers that behind the statistics are real human beings—flawed, needy, troubled, full of potential and deserving of understanding.

CHAPTER 1

Surviving on the Streets

The Lay of the Land

Tina S. and Jamie Pastor Bolnick

The following narrative is from the story of Tina S., a teenager who lived for four years in the tunnels beneath Grand Central Station in New York City.

Tina began living underneath the station when she was sixteen, although her living situation had been precarious for years before that. Her mother lived in a welfare hotel with an abusive man and several children, and many nights Tina did not go home. When she met April, another sixteen-year-old who lived in the tunnels, she and April became best friends, and they stayed together whenever one of them was not in jail or in the hospital—until two years later when April committed suicide.

In the passage that follows, Tina describes daily life in the tunnels, including how she found food, washed, made friends, and entertained herself. She also explains casually how important drugs and alcohol were in her life. Through most of the events related in the excerpt, her friend April was receiving mental health treatment at Elmhurst Hospital in New York City.

Years after the events related in this excerpt, Tina made a more stable life for herself. Wanting to piece together her own fragmented story, she sought out Jamie Pastor Bolnick, a journalist and photographer living in New York City, whom she had met when Bolnick was trying to write a book about April. To help Tina tell her story, Bolnick conducted hundreds of taped interviews with the people living beneath the station, as well as with experts in criminal justice and social services. She is also the author of Winnie: My Life in an Institution *(1985), and articles in* Redbook, Newsday *and other periodicals.*

For me, living in Grand Central Station was an adventure, the kind of crazy adventure kids have in library books.

Hunger was never a problem. A lot of churches had soup kitchens and you just had to know the schedules. On weekdays St. Michael's served breakfast and St. Joseph's served lunch and on Sundays they both also served dinner. During the week you could get dinner at the Salvation Army headquarters, or St. Catherine's on Lexington Avenue, or, on Fridays and Saturdays, at St. Andrew's. The Salvation Army also served holiday meals and so did some of the churches.

Also, seven nights a week both the Salvation Army and the Coalition for the Homeless sent food vans to Grand Central. At the Salvation Army van you could get a sandwich and hot soup, sometimes chili, and at the Coalition's you could get a sandwich and a pint of milk.

We'd hang out in Bryant Park all day. Play Frisbee, lie around on blankets in the sun, drink beer. Then when it was getting night we'd go back down to the abandoned train, drink beer, smoke reefer, and party half the night. Bonnie left in the middle of the summer because she was having R.J.'s baby, but she was back again a few weeks later. She had the baby, it was a boy, and she said some relative was taking care of it for her.

Cleaning Up

The only bad part was, living on a train you get kind of dirty. You could go wash your hands and face in the ladies' room sometimes, depending on which matron was on duty. Some were really bitchy, chased us out whenever they saw us.

Even when I did get to wash in the ladies' room, the rest of me was getting pretty ripe. The weather was warm and we were out running around Bryant Park getting sweaty and grubby. Then you'd go down to the train and you'd get dirty and sooty from climbing around the tracks. I was looking like a ragamuffin. I was smelling. Getting to the point where even washing my face and hands didn't help much.

The third week I was there, Bonnie took me down to the back of one of the tracks and showed me where she washed. It was a big old silver washbasin, and it was for the workers, but once in a while you could sneak in there if they weren't around. Take off all your clothes and climb in the sink. It was almost as good as taking a real bath. By the time I got out the water was all black.

There was a shower, too, that we used once in a while. It was down in one of the work areas on the lower level, and Francisco took me there. It was just a pipe with running water, but it was high up, so you could stand under it like a real shower. The workmen stored stuff down there, pipes and barrels and big bags of concrete, and that's also where they kept their forklift carts. You had to be careful nobody was around. Usually you could only go on a Sunday. We didn't have soap or towels or even clean clothes, we'd just put our dirty stuff back on afterwards. Or maybe throw away the top layers, like the sweatshirts or flannel shirts. It was the top layers that got the dirtiest, anyway.

Chewie, the cousin of Jabba, took me to his home in the South Bronx one night. It was mostly abandoned buildings there, and the house where his family lived was the only house still in one piece. Chewie told me to wait outside and he came out about half an hour later with a pair of jeans, a denim shirt, and some socks that belonged to one of his brothers. Chewie also had a bag of food: chicken wings and a jar of pickles and a couple apples.

Chewie was really good-looking, dark-skinned, curly hair, maybe eighteen years old. He's the guy I liked most when I first came. He was the type who would hold the door open for a girl.

"We All Get Bugs"

I was starting to itch a lot. Sometimes I'd be scratching so much it was hard to sleep, and I noticed I was getting little pink bumps, like bites, on my arms.

One Sunday I was stripping down to take a shower and feeling really itchy under my bra, and when I took it off I saw teeny little bugs crawling around the band. I picked one off, pinched it between my fingers, and it popped. I hollered, "Aaaagh!" and Francisco, who was standing guard by one of the forklifts, said, "What happened?"

I just said, "Oh, shit," because I realized my whole bra was infested. I threw it behind a stack of barrels and never wore a bra again, the whole time I was at Grand Central.

Only that didn't get rid of the bugs. It turned out they were all over me. Even showering didn't get them off. Francisco told Maria, because I was too ashamed, and she stole me some stuff from a drugstore that you put all over yourself to kill them. She said, "Don't feel bad, we all get bugs."

Even after that, I still had some left. Mostly in my hair. I just kept plucking them out whenever I felt them on my scalp. That's how I finally got rid of them all.

A New Friend Arrives

The whole time April was in Elmhurst, I lived on the abandoned train. I spoke to her almost every day on the phone, and she'd tell me funny stuff about some of the crazies on her ward. Always before we hung up she'd say, "Now, you're going to stay there until I come back, right?" I was so flattered she wanted me to wait for her, the station could have burned down and I wouldn't have budged.

Corey showed up around the end of summer. How we all met is when Chewie's cousin Jabba stole his wallet. Corey was in the men's room and he laid his wallet down on the sink, and Jabba, who was hanging out in there looking for something to steal, pocketed it. Corey was a good-looking, light-skinned black, and sweet, but he wasn't too bright or he never would have left his wallet on the sink.

I didn't even know at that time what Jabba had done, but I saw this cute young guy wandering around the waiting room and, maybe because we were all about the same age, he came over and told us his wallet was just stolen off the sink in the men's room.

He said, "Any of you guys know who could've taken it?" He was mostly asking Jabba, I guess, because he had seen him in there.

Jabba said, "No, man, but you ought to know better than to leave your valuables lying around when you're in New York City. I can tell you're an out-of-towner."

Corey said yeah, he was just up from Georgia and he wanted to go back because he tried New York and he didn't like it. Only now he couldn't leave because all his money was gone. So Maria and Francisco told him to go out on the main concourse and panhandle and he'd have enough money in no time.

Corey did make some money, because a few hours later he came back and asked, "Where do I buy the ticket?"

"What do you want a ticket for?" Jabba said. "Let's go get some beers."

Corey said okay, and we also got some reefer, and that night when we went down to the train we took Corey with us because now he had no money left for a ticket home and no place to sleep. The next day Jabba gave him back his wallet, without the money, of course. Said he found it in a trash can in front of the station. Corey was really grateful, he kept saying over and over, "Oh, wow, you found my wallet, man, thank you!"

That's how Corey started hanging out with us, and pretty soon he was mostly sticking around me. First it was me and Chewie and Corey and then it was just me and Corey, and after a while Corey got to be my boyfriend. You know that cartoon dog, Marmaduke? Corey was a little like that. Kind of clumsy and sweet at the same time. He would do whatever I wanted, and his feet were real big, so that made him awkward. Corey and me, we got to be a team. If we weren't together, we always knew where the other one was.

He wanted us to have sex but I told him, "Well, Corey, I'm not ready, I want to wait until I get to know you better." Corey was always gentlemanly and he let it be my decision.

Angel Dust

Corey introduced me to angel dust. He did a lot of it down in Georgia. It's green, it looks like leaves and smells like mint and it comes in a little bag, like pot. You roll it like pot, you take just two smokes and you're floating.

I thought it was great. When you smoke dust you feel like you can be anything or do anything. Corey told me about this one guy who jumped off a garage because he thought he could fly. Corey also told me you have to be careful because it can be very dangerous. On a dust high you could do something and not realize you did it, you could even kill somebody and not know it. And if you smoke too much, Corey said, you can forget who or where you are forever.

The Deepest Levels

They say there are seven levels below Grand Central, but no one I know has been that far down. Most people stay on the first level, right below the station's lower level. You just walk along the tracks until you find a place where you can crawl under the platform.

It's not too hard to get to the second level either, because if you know where to look, there are some old stairs and passages that the workmen use. But I went down to the third level with Corey and I'll never forget it.

He was telling me one day how he went exploring way deep, around the third or fourth level, and came across some guys living in boxes in a big cave. They even had a campfire. I heard that the deeper down you go, the weirder the people are. I heard stories about people who live so deep in the dark tunnels that skin has grown over their eyes, and about a man who'd lived down there for thirty years who cooks and eats the bodies of other bums he's murdered.

But I didn't think any of that stuff was true and I didn't believe what Corey said, either. I told him, "You're full of shit about those guys."

"No, I swear. I watched them. They don't talk, they make train noises. And one of them saw me, so I had to run."

"What'd he do? Toot his whistle?"

"You don't believe me, I'll show you. I can find that cave again."

I told him no way was I going down there. "Ten bucks," he said. "I pay you ten if I'm lying, you pay me ten if I prove it's true." Well, hell. For ten dollars.

I followed him down the tracks, and we crawled under the platform and through a big hole where the bricks had been moved away. I could hear steam hissing somewhere, from hot pipes, but it was totally dark. This was way below the boiler room, a place I'd never been. I said, "Wait, Corey, because I can't see," but he told me in a couple of minutes my eyes would adjust, and they did.

I think we were on the second level now. Corey had found a back way to get to it, without using the stairs. I followed him down a passage that was so low in some spots we had to crawl, and then we came to an even bigger hole in the side of the passage. It was weird because this hole was not supposed to be there, it was like somebody chipped it away or busted it out with a sledgehammer.

Lost in the Tunnels

Corey climbed through and I followed, and we came into a huge empty space full of rocks and boulders. It was like a big cavern. Except I could hear trains. No matter where we went, I could hear the trains above us through all those layers of rock and concrete, blowing their whistles and roaring up and down the tracks like monsters.

In order to get into the next passage, we had to walk along a high ledge, then climb down a rock and drop about eight feet. After we'd been walking and crawling for a while, I noticed a pile of rocks that I was sure I saw before.

I said, "Hey, Corey, I think we're going in circles."

He said, "No we're not, trust me."

When we passed the same pile of rocks again fifteen minutes later, I told him, "See? See? This is where we just were."

I was getting creeped out. We doubled back all the way to the cavern and got into a different passage, with little lights in the wall every hundred yards or so. I wondered, Do these bulbs ever burn out? And if they do, who keeps changing them?

At the end was a big hunk of flattened cardboard and a blanket, some clothes, beer cans, old newspapers, candles. Somebody's spot. That's when I really got scared. Because who knows what kind of nut was living here, and if the guy happened to come along and see us, he'd probably think we were there to steal his stuff. People like that, there's no way of knowing what they're going to do.

I grabbed Corey's sleeve, told him, "Listen, you won the bet, okay? Let's just get out of here."

I think he was relieved; he didn't know where the hell he was going, anyway. It took us over an hour to find our way back up to the first level. I heard stories of people getting lost down there. Most find their way back, but a few never do.

I never went below the first level again and I don't think Corey ever did, either.

April Returns

One day around the end of August, me and Corey were on the lower level smoking dust when Chewie came running down. "Yo, Tina," he said, "guess what, April's back!"

There was a big commotion when I got up to the waiting room. April was running around hugging everybody, hollering, "I'm home! I'm home!" I was so happy I almost couldn't believe she was real. She gave me a big hug and said, "Well, I'm glad to see you waited like I told you to!"

Turned out the hospital didn't let her go, she escaped. Her mom took her out to a restaurant and April told her she was going to the bathroom. Her mom said, "I know you're leaving. Just do it when I'm not looking." April said, "Okay. Bye," and walked out.

I took her down to the lower level and introduced her to Corey and he gave her some dust. We all got high together. She loved the dust, thought it was the best thing she ever had. So after that we were on a dust mission for months.

Sometimes, on dust, you can pretend you're in a different part of the world and it works. One time April, Corey, and me went to China, because it was April's turn to pick and that was the one place she said she really wanted to see.

Christmas on the Streets

Janice Erlbaum

In the narrative that follows, writer Janice Erlbaum tells her story of spending Christmas on the streets the year she turned fifteen. Erlbaum had left home because her mother would not break ties with an abusive husband, and she had been living in a homeless shelter for a month. Her narrative shows both the anxieties faced by young people who live this way and the tentative sense of community they can develop through sharing difficult experiences.

Erlbaum's narrative is excerpted from a book-length memoir, Girlbomb, *which follows the author from the day in 1984 that she walked out of her mother's home to the day almost three years later when she took possession of the keys to her own apartment. The story of that first Christmas began in mid-December, when the residents of the homeless shelter in the Hell's Kitchen section of New York City had been given a gift of new winter clothes. Erlbaum, still feeling proud and trying to impress the others, refused to wear the coat she had been given because she did not like the style, but she found that she was too cold in her denim jacket. As she reports, she was still attending high school—although rather half-heartedly—while she was living in the shelter, and she worried that when her allotted thirty days in the shelter ran out she would be placed in a group home far from her school. Although she had plans to earn a GED certificate and get a job, she found that she was too young to do either, and that her school guidance counselor was not able to offer much help.*

Erlbaum's housemates were in similarly challenging situations. Roxanne, for example, was also trying to complete high school, and Cookies and the angry and violent Sherri were preg-

nant. Erlbaum says that most of her housemates did not like her, and that there were too many rules. On Christmas Eve, however, the shelter became something like a home. There was a big turkey dinner and a few gifts, and when Erlbaum, Roxanne and a few other girls went out to see the tree at Rockefeller Center, the author found that even though she was determined not to enjoy it, she could not ignore the beauty and the feeling of companionship.

Erlbaum survived her years of homelessness, survived sex- and drug abuse, and is now a novelist, a poet, and a columnist for BUST magazine. She has also worked as a stand-up comic. She still lives in New York City, and teaches jewelry making in the homeless shelter in which she once lived.

Mid-December, and tinsel wreaths hung all over Times Square. Drunks yelled "Meh Kissmiss!" as they shoved their worn cups in your face. It was snowy, cold, and dark by five. My feet were consistently wet. I didn't have a winter coat. I'd walked out of my mother's apartment wearing my denim jacket over a sweater, and that was what I was still wearing, every day, until people couldn't help but notice.

"Aren't you cold?" asked Alice, stomping her feet and frowning as we smoked on the corner before school.

Hope stomped and frowned beside her. "Dude, you definitely need a new jacket."

Yes, *apparently*. But I'd refused the ugly doofus winter coat they offered everybody free at the shelter—I took the free socks, underwear, and sweatshirts, plus some donated sweaters that were kind of cool, in a retro way, but I was not going to walk around in public in an ugly doofus shelter coat. I'd rather freeze in my denim jacket, with its safety pins and marker scrawls and cigarette smell. And I kept planning to get myself something warmer at the Salvation Army, maybe a men's overcoat.

"Yeah . . . I'm probably going to get one this weekend. I have to Christmas shop anyway."

Hope and Alice swapped looks, like, Christmas shop? Who was I kidding? I ignored the looks and regarded the toe of my sneaker, twisting as it crushed the butt of a cigarette.

I *was* going shopping. For [my brother] Jake, if no one else. I had money. I still had some in the bank from my old cashier job. And I was going to get another job, too, it was part of my new plan: drop out of school, get my GED, become a secretary or something, and get my own place. Even if I had to be a cashier full-time, at five dollars an hour, that was still two hundred a week, eight hundred a month—I could make it work. I could get a room at the Y, or one of the flophouse hotels in Hell's Kitchen. The Hotel Mansfield Hall had semiprivate bathrooms, and they didn't care if you had a small fridge and a hot plate; I asked. Of course, the place was crawling with jittery freaks. And the guy in the Plexiglas booth in the lobby gave me the hairy eyeball.

"Aren't you a little young?" he asked, folding his meaty arms over his greasy T-shirt.

"No," I said, insulted, like when I got carded at bars, like, *how dare anyone question my maturity*? "I'm nineteen, I have my ID at home."

"Uh-huh."

The guy didn't buy it. Well, f--- him, "a little young." I could go down the block to Fascination on Broadway and get a fake ID for five dollars, they'd make it say I was sixty-three if I wanted. What did that prove? Age was just a number. I was already on my own, looking out for myself, more grown-up than any grown-up I knew. So what if I was only fifteen?

My guidance counselor, Ms. Glass, shook her frizzy head at me. "Hon, you're only fifteen! You're too young to take the GED. You've got to stay in school or you're a delinquent. It's the law."

I sat in her plastic chair and felt my throat close, tears of frustration forming. "But listen, Ms. Glass, I have to move out of the shelter, because I've been there more than thirty days, and you're only supposed to be there thirty days, and they keep saying they don't know where I'm going to go, and I'm just trying to . . . to take care of myself, to survive, you know?"

She didn't get it either. "Hon, you can*not* take care of yourself, you're too young! You have to work with them at the shelter to find you a placement. You can't live on your own!" She barked—*hah!*—and shook her head some more. "For god's sake, you're my daughter's age."

Well, what the f--- that had to do with anything, I didn't know. Ms. Glass was seriously no help to me at all. As a matter of fact, Ms. Glass was a useless dingbat, and her stupid pig daughter could go f--- herself too. I left her office and slipped quietly out the back entrance of the school, headed for Washington Square Park, done with school for the day.

I'd been at the shelter for about six weeks, almost two weeks past the deadline, and they still hadn't found me a bed. I didn't fully understand what was going on behind the scenes with my case. When I asked, the counselors told me, "We should have something for you soon. Just hang tight."

There was a lot of comparison shopping among the girls waiting for placement. Some people knew a lot more than I did about the various options. Foster care was the worst, they agreed—a girl named Yvette told me, "They just stick you with whatever stranger they got, like a dog from the pound. You don't even know them. They could be real strict, too. It's worse than living at home. I ran away twice from foster homes. F--- that. I'm trying to get into a group home, otherwise, I don't know. They could arrest me, I'm not going back to foster care."

Group homes were supposed to be better than foster care, but they were also supposed to be strict, especially the religious ones. I'd heard from the start that they were thinking of sending me to a group home, and I knew Roxanne was in line for one, too.

"This place is bad enough, I'm not going to live in some convent," I told Roxanne, huddling next to her on a stoop. "I don't care. I'll go live with my boyfriend from school." He didn't technically exist yet but would surely materialize any day.

Roxanne was more practical. "I just want someplace where I can still get to my school. They're talking about putting me way out in Brooklyn, in Canarsie—that's too far. I don't want to switch out of my school. And how'm I supposed to get to you from Canarsie?"

I leaned into her and pushed her with my shoulder. She pushed back. We did this a lot—pushed each other, leaned on each other—to punctuate a comment. Sometimes we just stayed arm to arm, mooshing against each other in a kind of Greco-Roman shoving match. Then I'd go to light a cigarette, and she'd push me away, coughing exaggeratedly and waving her hand in front of her face.

"Well, I have to find something soon. I'm past thirty days here. They could throw me out anytime."

Roxanne pooh-poohed this. "They're not throwing you out. If they were gonna throw you out, you'd have *been* thrown out. They're probably gonna send you to a group home, and they're just waiting to see where a bed opens up."

Easy for her to say. She had ten whole days until her deadline, and nobody was actively trying to beat her ass. I pulled away and lit a cigarette. "I'm just saying, they better find me something soon."

Roxanne leaned over and smooshed me. "You'll be all right."

I wasn't so sure. Roxanne wasn't home much these days, between school and her new job—things were changing at the shelter, and not for the better. My nemesis Sherri was still there, way past her own deadline, waiting for a bed to open up in one of the scarce group homes for teen mothers. Now seven months pregnant, she was angrier than ever, slamming into walls and beating her legs with her fists, pounding her hand down at the dinner table to make the plates jump.

"That f---ing white bitch make me so sick I can't even eat!"

Everybody around her at the far end of the table laughed. Sister Thomas Rita glared at them.

"We will have *none* of that," she ordered. "I will give everybody a warning."

Stuff like this made things nine or ten times worse for me. Now Sherri was a nun's bitch, on top of the already established racist, snitch, cracker, and ho.

Sherri had lost the support of my erstwhile roommate Treece, but now she was backed by two newer girls, Earletta and Cookies. Earletta was tall and mean, and she asked upon first sight of me, "What *her* white ass is doing here?"—not in a friendly, interested way, either. Cookies was short and pregnant, and equally militant in her approach. Together, the three of them went out of their way to make my life suck.

If I put something down and left the room, that thing was gone. My chem book, my fresh pack of cigarettes, my sweater. I kept my shoes on at all times; I couldn't afford to lose them. And if Earletta wanted to come up right behind me in the TV room and literally breathe all over the back of my neck, I had to sit there and pretend that it wasn't happening, or that it didn't bother me.

"Whatever you want to do," I muttered to myself.

"You say something to me, white girl?"

Nothing. Just kept watching the TV like there wasn't nasal slobber on me.

It wasn't just the three of them, either; it was the whole house. Popular sentiment had shifted against me, not that it had ever shifted toward me at any point, and whatever status I might have once had as a novelty—See how white girl looks with cornrows! Watch white girl dance—had worn off. Even Baby Vondell didn't love me anymore, or not in public, anyway. Sometimes when nobody was around, she'd still latch on to my arm. "Mamma, you wanna hear about my new boyfriend? His name's Justice, and he's so fine, he a real proud black man . . . Mamma, you got a cigarette for me?" Then ten minutes later she'd be blowing smoke in my face, laughing at me.

Roxanne wasn't catching most of this, and if she did, there wasn't much she could say. She wasn't afraid to defend me; she just knew, as I did, that it would only make things worse. She'd heard that she was on her way out, shipping off to the group home in Canarsie right after New Year's. That was almost two hours away from her school on the subway, but what was she going to do?

More to the point, what was *I* going to do?

At least Christmas Eve at the shelter was festive—raucous, even, in the overheated house, but genially so, because there was an extra-big meal of fresh turkey and ham and all good holiday things, plus extra desserts. Everybody got three dollars cash, and they were giving us gift bags and having entertainment after curfew. It was a rare good night to be at the shelter.

"Where's Vondell?" asked Sister Thomas Rita, counting heads at the dinner table. "Has anybody seen Vondell?"

Quietly, from the end of the table: "Seen her suckin' a dick on Tenth Ave." Snickers, muffled by the general din.

"Sister, I di'nt seen her, but if she miss her curfew tonight, she said I could take her shampoo."

Somebody muttered, "Dumb bitch is missing out, because this food is for real."

No kidding. Turkey and gravy, sweet potatoes and stuffing, green beans and cranberry sauce—this was *food.* Not the frozen spinach and Cream of Wheat we usually made do with. I took myself another helping of everything. Too bad for Vondell.

After dinner, me and Roxanne and a few other girls lugged over to Rockefeller Center to look at the tree. I had planned to be unimpressed—so what, it was a *dead tree*—but it turned out to be pretty spectacular, the sheer mammoth size of it, twinkling like an arcade game.

"Damn," said VeeVee, her head tipped all the way back to her neck. "That shit is real?"

All of Fifth Avenue was lit with white lights, all of Central Park South. Well-dressed people came out of the hotels, rode by in carriages, smiling and looking happy. There was a sparkling fresh coat of snow on the ground, and the night was crisp and thrilling on our faces.

"It is so beautiful tonight." Roxanne turned to smile at me, wet-eyed. "I can't believe it."

I reached out my hand. She took it and put both our hands in her pocket, pulling me close alongside her.

Back at the house, there was cocoa with little marshmallows in it, but *real* little marshmallows—not the dehydrated package kind—left over from the sweet potatoes. Then they gave us all gift bags. Inside were sweaters, some nail polish and lipstick, and these educational video games that nobody had a player for. The video games got tossed around the TV room and mostly ended up under the couch, as everyone shrieked and started their manicures.

One gift bag sat unclaimed—Baby Vondell still had not returned. Now she had blown her curfew by two hours, and girls were excited.

"Where she at?"

"She think they not gonna discharge her because it's Christmas Eve?"

"That's some messed up shit, if a nun throw you out in the snow on Jesus' birthday."

"So what? That bitch ain't the Virgin Mary."

Roxanne offered me her tube of Lady Ebony lipstick. "Here, make yourself look nice for a change." I mooshed her, and she sat on me. Sherri cut her eyes at us and stage-whispered to Cookies. *F---in' dykessss.*

The entertainment that night, besides Vondell's absence, was three hippies with guitars playing Christmas carols and Beatles tunes. "This shit is corny," complained Yvette, but soon she was singing along to "Frosty the Snowman." The hippies stayed past midnight, way past the regular lights-out time, until the counselors finally broke it up and sent us to bed—bellies swollen, nails tacky with new paint, visions of secure housing dancing in our heads.

My Life as a Male Teen Prostitute

Aaron Kipnis

In the following viewpoint Aaron Kipnis looks back on his own teenage years when he lived on the streets or behind bars, and worked as a prostitute. Now a noted psychologist who has made a career of studying homeless and runaway teenage boys, he describes his past with stark clarity, revealing little emotion.

According to Kipnis, he was on the streets of Hollywood at a young age, too young to get an honest job to support himself. Instead, he broke into cars to steal food, spare change, and things to sell. At fifteen, he found that the only way to earn a steady income was to work as a prostitute. When Hollywood began to feel too dangerous, he says, he hitchhiked to San Francisco, and later to Los Angeles. Wherever he went, he found men willing to take advantage of him sexually. Kipnis comments that as an adult he realizes that American society is more willing to tolerate the sexual abuse of boys than of girls.

At seventeen, after some months as a ward of the state of California, Kipnis was homeless again. He worked as a dishwasher, and supplemented his diet with food left behind in restaurants and in dumpsters. Constantly hungry, he remembers, he began for the first time to consider selling drugs.

Aaron Kipnis is a national speaker and consultant on issues of male psychology, including the development of boys into men and the training of men to be good fathers. He is a member of the faculty at Pacifica Graduate Institute in Carpenteria, California, and the author of Knights Without Armor *(1991) and* Angry Young Men *(1999) from which this narrative is excerpted.*

Aaron Kipnis, *Angry Young Men: How Parents, Teachers, and Counselors Can Help "Bad Boys" Become Good Men.* Hoboken, NJ: San Francisco: Jossey-Bass, 1999.

When not behind bars, I spent most of my adolescence living in or near street life. I was usually broke. Survival took up a good portion of each day. I regularly looked for work but was repeatedly refused because of my age, few skills, and the lack of an address or phone number. Also, using only public bathrooms for hygiene, it was difficult to stay impeccably clean. I imagine my appearance got somewhat scruffy over time. The hungrier I got the more I fantasized about stealing as an immediate way to get food or money. Like most low-level offenders, I was not particularly violent. But I wanted to survive. So, I started committing petty thefts.

Armed with a coat hanger, I'd walk the streets of the Hollywood Hills late at night. Many cars were unlocked. Others I'd open with the hanger, sticking it down between the window and the door frame to catch the locks. Rifling cars produced a steady stream of spare change, an occasional item I could sell on the street, and often a place to sleep.

Though I always tried to wake before dawn, I preferred sleeping in underground garages where I could hear people approaching in the morning if I overslept. The few times someone discovered me, I bolted and ran, hopping fences and working my way through the tangles of poison oak, manzanita, honeysuckle, and sage that filled the rugged canyons below.

I was always quickly away and never caught. But for many years I was haunted by exhausting dreams about endlessly running away from pursuers. Once I snagged a doctor's bag, an item that suddenly elevated a petty theft to a serious felony. A junkie on the boulevard paid $20 for it, enough to support me for a week. Generally, however, these thefts were insufficient to even provide me with steady meals.

I never planned to get involved with prostitution. I simply drifted into it as I got more desperate. Hustling gay men proved to be the only steady income I could produce as a homeless fifteen-year-old. I "turned" my first "trick" at 4:00

A.M. in a Hollywood hotel. A man bought me drinks in a bar till 2:00, fed me steak at an all-night diner, and then took me to his room. He was a dumpy, pasty white guy with a wife and kids in the suburbs. So were many of the others along the way.

One day I met a guy on the Sunset Strip who took me to a large abandoned house in the hills. There, about ten gay men were squatting. They had turned the gas on at the street and were cooking a pot of stew over a gas log in the fireplace. The only furniture consisted of some mattresses lying around and a stained, threadbare couch rescued from some alleyway. I shared their meal. Gary let me sleep on the couch.

Because "you dance with whom you came" I "belonged" to Gary. The other guys left me alone. But there was a high-strung guy, Patrick (Patty), who kept asking for sex when Gary wasn't around. But Patty was a jerk and also had nothing to offer. So, I just kept putting him off. After all, sex was my only coinage at the time. I tried to only spend it for survival.

After a week or so Patty got agitated about being refused. Then he got aggressive. I fought him off, giving him a black eye. A few nights later I was at the After Hours club, where I often hung out and danced. During a break, I went out to the alley to cool off. A couple of dealers, who regularly sold drugs at the club, suddenly attacked me. Patty had told everyone that I was a police informant, doubly dangerous because I was a minor. The first part wasn't true. Though today I work professionally with law enforcement at times, I had nothing but contempt for the police at that stage of life. But I was banned from the club and the house, exiled to the street again.

A man who worked for Bank of America picked me up and took me to his apartment late that night. After being coerced into having sex with him, I became so distressed that I tried to slash my wrists with a razor blade in his bathroom. This was my third suicide attempt, having unsuccessfully overdosed with pills twice in recent years. I was unable to cut myself very deeply. I remember feeling like a coward. The bank teller discovered me bleeding in his bathtub; even those superficial cuts made quite a mess. He was furious. It was about 3:00 A.M. He taped up my wrists, made me get dressed, put me in the car, drove me back to Hollywood, and pushed me out of the door. I spent the rest of the night sitting in a twenty-four-hour diner drinking coffee.

Broke, bruised, depressed, and no longer feeling safe in Hollywood, I hitchhiked out of town the next morning. I caught rides up Highway 101 along the California coast, generally heading for San Francisco. A couple picked me up in Big Sur, took me in, fed me, tended my cuts, and shared their infinite supply of excellent pot. He was a burly, heavily bearded sculptor. His willowy, long-haired wife grew herbs, vegetables, and marijuana in a large organic garden. This was the first of many times in my life that I was blessed by unconditional compassion emanating from counter-cultural strangers. I worked around the house and garden for a few days, gained strength, and moved on.

A week of bumming my way up the coast brought me to San Francisco's Tenderloin district. After a few homeless days, two Hell's Angels offered me a place to crash. I moved into their single, $20-a-week room in a hotel near Turk and Eddy Streets. Betty, a teenaged runaway from Indiana, was also there. We slept in shifts, generally using the room at different times than the bikers.

Betty was also hustling for survival. We walked the streets and worked the clubs from about 10:00 P.M. until 2:00 or 3:00 in the morning. Sometimes we'd hang out together. But just like Hollywood, the straight and gay trolling grounds were on different streets, so we mostly had to go it alone. Then, unless we were spending the night with a trick, we'd come home and crash. We often held one another in the bed for comfort.

The two bikers were running a scam that kept them on the street from 3:00 A.M. until dawn. They had a key that opened parking meters. They would raid them in the small hours, coming back to the hotel room in the late morning to wrap coins after their breakfast, I'd get up then, hit the streets, and come back sometimes to sleep in the afternoon when the bikers were usually out.

I don't know why they let me live there. I found, as I made my way along the underground corridors of our culture, that outlaws were often unexpectedly kind. While the churches and synagogues barred their doors at night and my middle-class relatives just did not care, it was usually the poor, the outcast, the freaks, and the down-trodden who offered me a hand. They asked for little. More often than not, they asked for nothing in return.

My first night in San Francisco I slept in the bushes above the Union Street parking garage. It was a cold night. A raggedy alcoholic bundled up in the same hedge told me, "Hey, this is no place for a kid." He gave me a musty blanket he'd bundled under his head for a pillow and dug into his pocket for 50 cents. He told me to buy a bowl of soup in the diner across the street so as not go to sleep hungry. That was probably all the money he had. The blanket was half his personal property. Like Blanche, in *A Streetcar Named Desire*, I survived primarily because of the kindness of strangers. The generosity of this bum in the bushes touched me deeply. In my current good fortune the memory of him assures I do not forget those with less.

The bikers got busted one night. Cops came in the middle of the night. Betty and I were in the bed. They searched the place and hauled away coin wrappers as evidence. They asked us if we knew anything about an extra parking meter key. We said no, we just used the room to sleep when the guys weren't there—the truth. The cops left us there. Why they didn't haul us in, I'll never know. Betty took off for parts unknown the next day. I never saw her again.

I couldn't afford the next week's rent on the room so I moved in with two gay men down the hall, Jackie and Johnny. They taught me tricks of the street-hustling trade. It seemed like a good deal at the time. In addition to $10 or $20 in my pocket, sometimes a decent meal or a bath in a comfortable hotel also came along. Ten bucks equaled twenty chili-dogs or a week's rent-share for my Tenderloin firetrap. It wasn't until years later, when a friend's sister told me she made $500 a night hooking, that I realized my innocence was so cheaply sold. In a strange twist of "equity pay," boys don't command nearly as much for their bodies as girls. One day, as winter began to cool the streets, Jackie went off to Mexico. I hopped a Greyhound bus with Johnny and went back to Los Angeles in search of warmer nights.

I stayed away from the After Hours club. Patty had ruined my reputation there. But Johnny introduced me to new haunts in the arts and theater district of West Hollywood. The 8727 was an underground gay club on Melrose Avenue. Outside, nothing advertised its presence but the address. Inside, the flame of Hollywood gay culture burned with bright intensity.

We hustled a little but mostly just hung out. Night after night I reveled in the scene. Actors came in after the theaters closed. Intellectuals lit up the night with articulate debate. Drag queens preened occasionally, adding a campy hilarity to the night. And there was a steady stream of food, drugs, and lodging. The occasional payment of sex assured the older men who paid for it all that I was a player.

I spent nights drinking bottomless cups of coffee, chain smoking cigarettes inside and marijuana outside, dropping bennies (benzedrine) like M&M's, and talking with everyone about anything and everything. The richness, tempo, and depth I missed in school were abundant in the coffeehouses. I learned about art, music, poetry, literature, dance, cinema, sex, radical politics, and the engaging psychology of those living outside society's norms.

Like a vampire, I left before the full sun of first light, lest it somehow return me to the demon hells of depression stored behind the manic mask I wore in those nocturnal parades. The amphetamine-drenched nights heightened the mystical quality of dawn as I often walked to the boulevard for breakfast awash in beauty.

Abandoned as I was by straight culture, gay men kept me alive. But they also took their toll. Some tricks abused me, cheated me, gave me disorienting drugs, pressured or threatened me. I often felt afraid of things getting out of control. On two occasions, "gay bashers" (men who beat homosexuals for sport) assaulted me.

Ironically, I never regarded myself as gay. Men have never sexually attracted me. Many adolescent male hustlers self-identify as heterosexuals. But since few women seek male prostitutes, street boys, gay or straight, work the gay clientele. In Los Angeles today, just as in my time thirty-five years ago, women still work the straight crowd on Sunset while boys walk the streets of Selma or Santa Monica, a few blocks south.

The gay scene was the most interesting subculture around till LSD hit town. The whole bizarre milieu intrigued me in some perverse way with a strange charm. It's taken a lifetime, however, to recover from the shame and sexual confusion resulting from some of these experiences as a teen prostitute.

During my street years I met numerous kids selling sex for food, lodging, or drug habits oft incurred to medicate the pain they felt as discards. It wasn't until I began working intensively with male clients, however, that I began to understand these experiences as sexual abuse.

Most people would immediately regard a homeless, teenaged girl prostitute as a victim of predatory adults. But I never thought about my life that way, in part because no one else ever framed it in that light. Like many victims of child sexual abuse who blame themselves, for years I felt that any deviance in my experience must have been my own. Although it is essential for people in recovery to take responsibility for their actions, it is also important for abuse survivors to understand the impacts predatory sex can have on their psyche. For most men and boys, however, this topic is so taboo and shame-laden, they rarely find forums supporting forthright discussions about the impact of uncomfortable, early sexual experiences.

Today, there is a serious drought of compassion for males. Cynicism abounds. I've conducted seminars in a number of mental health institutions with blatant double standards of care for young men. Recent research confirms, however, that at least one-third of all child sexual abuse, perpetrated by both women and men, is against boys. Yet many sex-abuse treatment programs still predominately focus on female victims and male abusers.

In California, legislators did not even make the statutory rape of boys illegal until 1993. Yet various studies and the stories many young men tell me indicate that sexual abuse creates as many psychological problems for boys as girls. When working with male clients I am still surprised at how often sexual abuse emerges from their personal histories. Few report, however, that anyone previously showed much concern about it.

To remedy this lacuna in psychological treatment theory and training, clinicians, educators, and other helping professionals may need education that better sensitizes them to the often silent suffering of boys. To even speak of males as victims, however, rubs against the dominant cultural grain. To get needed male sensitivity training on the agenda of our mental health and educational institutions, our culture must confront its apathy toward the often hidden vulnerability and pain of angry young men.

Today, thousands of boys continue to walk the nation's streets with little support from social services. It isn't until they become bad boys, until they attract the interest of the criminal justice system, that most of these boys get any significant attention. For many of them, by the time they get into juvenile justice, it's too late. What does it say about our society that we cavalierly abandon thousands of boys to prostitution, drug addiction, AIDS, and the violence that accompanies life on the streets?. . .

My second major homeless period started after I turned seventeen, and the California Youth Authority released me as an emancipated minor. I rented a cheap apartment in the same part of Hollywood I'd worked as a prostitute two years earlier. About six months later, however, I lost my job as a county clerk and started washing dishes at a trendy French restaurant on the Sunset Strip.

I was stunned by the quantity of food wealthy diners left on their plates. This was my first ongoing encounter with affluent adults, or, at least, their leftovers. Steaks that skinny women hardly touched, half-finished lobster tails, mounds of salad, whole baked potatoes, and piles of vegetables filled the plates sent back to me for cleaning.

I lined my coat pockets with plastic and stuffed them nightly with leftovers. That fed me during off-work hours as well as my unemployed roommate and other kids I knew living on the fringes of Hollywood. I was appalled that the restaurant wasted so much expensive food. I realized then that wealthy people lived in an entirely different universe of privilege.

One of my most visceral memories from the street years is one of persistent hunger. I'd go into fast food restaurants and finish food left on tables, glean garbage cans, and retrieve discarded sand sharks from fishermen at the Venice pier. Shark stew was pretty good. Even a small shark, combined with vegetables plucked from a supermarket dumpster, would feed a lot of kids.

I had a whimsical moment, years later, while visiting my publisher's home near Beverly Hills, following the release of my first book. Earlier that day, a limousine provided by a television talk show had driven me around town. As I relaxed, sipping Perrier and listening to jazz in the air-conditioned embrace of the limo's plush interior, I felt strangely amused as we passed through the same streets where I once struggled.

In my mind, I waved to that skinny boy on the streets and told him to take heart, that the wheel of life kept turning and many delightful surprises were ahead. He just had to persevere and keep hope alive. That evening, my publisher told me he had occupied his exquisite home for over thirty years. I realized that he had once been on my Wednesday night trash-picking route. But not wishing to spoil an enchanting dinner with a sordid tale, I just kept this story to myself, as with most of these memoirs, until now.

Even with the free food gathered from the restaurant, a dishwasher's wages were insufficient to pay rent and other expenses. But I didn't want to go back to hustling. I was fiercely heterosexual at this point, with a girlfriend, April, living in a Bahai faith foster home nearby. And, in part from encountering so much sexual violence in jail, the thought of sex for cash now felt humiliating and repulsive. So, I closed that door. But I still needed more money. "Opportunities" to sell drugs, which I had previously declined, started looking more attractive.

Abuse at Home Leads
to Life on the Street

New Statesman & Society

According to various estimates, between 300,000 and 600,000 children in the United States work as prostitutes. The following viewpoint by a young girl named Cindy tells how she ran away from an abusive home life and ended up a homeless, heroin-addicted prostitute at the age of fifteen.

According to Cindy, she and her siblings were neglected and abandoned by her mother, and physically abused by her father. This abuse from her parents led her to run away. At first, she thought the freedom was great, but soon that freedom led to homelessness, drug abuse, and prostitution.

At the time this article was written, Cindy still had not gotten help. She was still addicted to heroin and still resorting to prostitution for money. She claimed that she had no incentive to get her act together, even though she knew that finding a normal job and getting clean would be best for her.

Cindy, a prostitute with a heroin habit who started living rough at 15, now has a relatively secure home. But, she explains, her other problems seem to be here to stay.

How It All Began

It started when I was young. My dad was married to my mum, my real mum, and I had a brother who's a year older than me. Then they had another child my younger brother. They were living in a really deprived flat. My dad was doing DJ-ing, on and off, so he was drinking a lot in the clubs. And my mum and dad didn't get on.

My mum really did neglect us, she used to lock us in the bedroom and didn't feed us or anything—she used to leave us in our nappies [diapers] all day. It got to a stage where my little brother started having convulsions because he really wasn't getting looked after. So social services were brought in, and they had a watchful eye over us from a very young age.

Then my mum and dad got divorced. They just weren't getting on, and there was a lot of violence at home. My dad started drinking heavily, he wasn't working, so he was just trying to make ends meet. Then he met this other woman who already had a child of her own, and after the divorce was through they got married. She was all for her kids and not for my dad's. She favoured hers over us and was really neglecting my younger brother, who was very ill at the time. He was still suffering from bad eczema, dehydration and convulsions. She literally made his life a misery. He was really poorly as a child. He was also really withdrawn, because he was so ill and badly treated. It was horrendous.

Abused by an Alcoholic Father

We used to get regular beatings off my dad, who was always drunk, and he used to beat my stepmum up a lot. He used to kick her down the stairs, and he was really ill. I remember one night my dad was due in and he'd slept out with another woman all night. My stepmum woke me up and she says, "Right, I'm going to get this bastard," for what he'd done. She smashed bottles outside so if he was really drunk he'd fall on them. That was her idea of revenge. Anyway, that night he brutally beat her, and beat us all up as well. He got arrested and placed in custody for it.

Then my dad didn't ever come back and just left us all there. My mum kidnapped my younger brother and took him to my nana's where she was staying. Then my older brother, who didn't like my stepmum at all, left of his own accord. I stayed there for six weeks, and then I went to stay with my dad.

Actually we got on quite well, but then he met this other woman who was only a couple of years older than me. I was having a really rough time accepting her after I'd been the role model of a mother for quite a long time, bringing my younger brothers up with my dad. I think I tried to mess it up for them, although there was a spell when they split up and I helped them get back together.

I'd been having a really rough time with my dad. I'd just started secondary school and I had a really horrible uniform. I didn't like to be in school and I couldn't settle to my work. I was always scribbling in my books and ripping them up. It was just after Christmas, and my dad had bought me a keyboard for a present. I sold it, and I was really scared to go home and tell my dad what I'd done. I was really frightened of what might happen. If I was two minutes late home, I used to get leathered, 'cause my dad wouldn't believe that the bus was late.

Honestly, there were stages where I had black eyes, marks and bruises, broken ribs and burst blood vessels on my face. My dad was really violent. I couldn't understand why, because we were just kids. And because I never had any money to buy things, I sold my keyboard. It was a 60 [pound] thing and I sold it for a fiver. It was a lot of money to me. I bought every-one in class ice-cream. But then I was really frightened of my dad and I put myself in care.

Running Away

I went into a children's home, but they kept sending me back home when I didn't want to go because the violence was at its peak. They were making every excuse they could: you can make it work, everything'll be fine, and it never was. It was always the same and I didn't like my dad's new wife. I just couldn't accept why she was there.

I kept running away from the home. I suppose I caused a lot of problems but they weren't intentional, I just wanted to do what I wanted to do. Be a kid, do things that kids do, get up to mischief and all that. So I was running wild. I was mad, I blew cars up in garages, with lads. I used to put matches in petrol cans. I thought it was great, but now I think it's silly. I'd never seen anything like that before. Because my dad had been so strict with me, I'd never had any freedom. It was brilliant.

In the end they put me in a secure unit, but I escaped from that by climbing over barbed wire in my nightie. I just wanted to get away and make a break for freedom after being locked up like that. The only thing I did to make myself a bit normal was to bury myself in my work and that's when I did all my exams. I did them at 14 and again at 15, GCSE [General Certificate of Secondary Education] level. I did really well. That was my way, I was burying myself in my work. I was always in the top class. I had a thirst for knowledge when I was in there, I used to love it.

Every time I absconded, I ran away to Manchester. There was just this one lad that I was really in love with, and all the time I was locked up I was thinking, I've got to get back to him. He was living with his mates. They were all 18. I was very young, but I was an old 14 so they accepted me in their group. I suppose in a way I was a bit of a slag. It was the only security I knew, sex was really new to me then. That was the only sort of closeness I ever got with men, after all the violence at home. Obviously I was being used. I was being taken advantage of because I was easy. But I didn't know at the time that was what was happening. I just thought, this is great, I'm getting a bit of attention.

The last time I ran away from the home, I just never went back. They said, well fair enough, you make your own way.

And that was it. I was totally cut off from everybody. My family didn't want to know, social workers weren't interested, nobody was interested. It was just me then, left in this big wide world. So I made my own way and I made myself a lot wiser. I lived through experiences that most people probably never go through in their lives. I've been absolutely poverty-stricken and during some of my younger years, like 15, 16, I really was living rough, I didn't change my clothes for days.

Life with Nicky

And then I met my boyfriend. Nicky. But we were still homeless. We wanted to be together and the hostels wouldn't take us together, it was one of us in one hostel, one in another. But we desperately wanted to be together and that was how we were going to stay.

We were living with his sister, with his friends, we were living rough, we were living anywhere we could get a bed for the night. Not necessarily the same bed for more than one night running. It was like anyone who'd have us and they were getting really pissed off with us at one stage. Nicky ruined a lot of good friendships through me that he'd had since he was younger because people didn't mind taking him, but both of us was a bit much.

Prostitution

The only money I was getting was through Nicky, he was making a bit of money here, a bit of money there. He was doing a bit of thieving, a bit of burgling. But then I started as a prostitute last year, last Christmas. I was sort of drawn into it by seeing girls with loads of money. Some of them were only 14, or 15, and they were earning like a hundred quid. And I thought to myself, oh, this could be a good thing.

Nicky had a heroin habit at that time and his addiction was quite strong. He had no money to buy gear and he was withdrawing. So I decided that I'd do a punter, you know, to get money for gear. I was about 15 at the time. It was a spur of the moment thing, Nicky was withdrawing, there was money to be made and I didn't have really much time to mess about. I was doing punters every day from then on. It was always the same routine. I've been quite lucky really, because up till now I haven't been hurt. Luckily, a lot of my punters were regulars, and they liked me because I was easy-going. I didn't push them, I didn't rush them, I just gave them good service.

Some of them become really attached to you, they become like really good friends. I like them as people and I think that's what Nicky doesn't understand, but I can't help it because I love people, people that are good to me, people that help me out. It's not always business. Some of them just like to be near you, like a bit of company, it's your friendship, your loyalty, your understanding. A lot of the time I do switch off as far as the sex bit of it's concerned. It's a case of having to, because I don't want a relationship with them and I don't feel anything sexual for them.

I just want to get by in life and if prostitution's the only way for me to keep my boyfriend out of jail and to keep me in things that I need, then that's how I'll go about it. At 15 and 16 I wasn't getting any state benefits at all, so it was prostitution or starvation. It was an alternative to starvation and dirty clothes and nowhere to live. Prostitution really was a last resort because I couldn't get a job at that age, and YTS [Youth Training Scheme] money wouldn't have got me through a day. I just couldn't make ends meet with state benefits, or college money. With prostitution, I can earn more in a night than state benefits give me in a month.

Drugs

I first started using drugs because I was buying them for Nicky. I wanted a way out and he seemed to be all right. He was using his drugs, that was his way out, and I was spending so much money on drugs and getting nothing in return, I thought, hell, I'm going to have some, I'm paying for it.

So I just started havin a little smoke at flint, you know, just the odd line here and the odd line there. But if you use on a regular basis, no matter how much you use, you're building up a tolerance for it and you need a little bit more everyday. I carry on doing what I'm doing because I can't see any break in life from it at the moment. What's the point in stopping it? I don't want to be a prostitute if I'm not on drugs, so I'm just going to be skint again if I stop taking drugs. I'd just be back to square one again. I'd just be the same boring Cindy: problems, no money, no job.

Drugs just seem to be the answer to me. I think this is my way of saying, well I'm coping with it, maybe not in the best of ways, but I don't starve, I never go hungry, my clothes aren't always filthy. I can't base anything on a future, because the way the economy is at the minute, I don't know if there's going to be anything for me.

A Typical Day

A typical day for me is, like, I get up, I won't even get out of bed until I've had a hit if I'm injecting. If I'm smoking, I have a smoke. I'll have a bath, wash my hair, put my make-up on, get ready to go round on the beat and meet the punters if I've got any to meet. I get my Durex [brand of condoms] sorted out, put my bag in order and then I'll go out on the beat. I'll do my first punter. If I can get 25 [pounds] or more I'll go to score again, or have a second smoke or injection.

And then back again. I try my best after that to not score again until I'm going home and then I've got to find at least 70 [pounds], that's after scoring twice in a day as well as the morning, because I need 25 [pounds] for the night, 25 [pounds] in the morning and possibly 20 [pounds], 25 [pounds] to pay off any debts, food for that day and the day after. Then I go home, have a final fix or final smoke and sit about bored 'cause our telly's been stolen.

Nicky and I have been in and out of hostels and various other places like refuges and friends and all that. But really this home that we've got now is the first proper home we've had since we got back together last Christmas. The place we're in now is like our place now, it's our home and that's all we've got. It's not much, but we've got a cooker, a fridge, we've got hot water, heating, a bed, clothes. It's still not what we're aiming for, but at least it's something. It's nothing to a lot of people but it's a lot to me because it's bit of security for us, we're not sleeping rough. We might as well be for the state of the place, because we can't afford to furnish it, we can't afford to do anything with it at the moment.

"There's Just Nothing for Us"

We've just about got Christmas out of the way. We didn't have any money over Christmas, no presents, no cards, bit of a sad time really, because we didn't have anything. But hopefully things are going to pick up. I have been injecting for a while but lately I've been smoking. I've got myself off like, digging in if you like, and I've been smoking. Hopefully that'll influence Nicky to do the same. Maybe in the future we'll get off gear, but I can't plan anything while I'm on drugs, because there's nothing to plan for. There's no jobs, there's no money, there's nothing for us to work for. If I had a goal, believe me I'd work for it. I'd do anything to get a normal job, I really would. It'd be an incentive for me to stop taking drugs, to get my act together. At the moment there's just nothing for us.

My Friends Didn't Know
I Was Homeless

Sandy Fertman Ryan

In the following narrative a girl explains the shame associated with being homeless. Like many teens, she remained in school although she did not have a proper home, and she worked diligently to keep her classmates from learning that she lived in a shelter.

As the girl reports, she and her mother and younger brother moved to California from Mexico when she was six years old. When their housing plans fell through, the family turned to the Bible Tabernacle homeless shelter in the city of Venice, where the girl lived most of the next eleven years. The shelter was a firmly structured environment, with strict times for eating, showering, and praying, and she remembers that she could not do many of the normal social things her classmates were doing, like hanging out after school.

Still, she managed to make friends, including one close friend she refers to as Emily. But even Emily did not know that her friend was homeless, because the girl lied about the small details of her life. Finally, the narrator says, she did tell Emily her secret, and even had her friend over to spend the night. At the time she told her story to reporter Sandy Fertman Ryan, the girl was seventeen and heading to a community college. Her mother had found a good job and the family had a home.

Sandy Fertman Ryan has written for Seventeen *and* Teen *magazines, and is a regular contributor to* Girls' Life. *She has published several articles in which she has helped girls tell their own stories about sensitive topics including foster care, self-cutting, bulimia, and serious illness.*

Sandy Fertman Ryan, "Homeward Bound: True Story," *Girls' Life*, vol. 9, August–September 2002, pp. 66–67. Copyright 2002 GLAC. Reproduced by permission.

I was born in Mexico. I don't remember much about my first few years growing up there—just that life was really hard. My mom never had money, and there weren't any jobs. So when I was 6, my mom, little brother and I came to the United States. My mom wanted us to have a better life.

We moved to California, near Los Angeles. My mom thought she had a good place for us to live, but that didn't work out. Mom's only choice was to take us to a homeless shelter.

The afternoon we arrived at the Bible Tabernacle shelter, I was so scared. The shelter was dark and crowded with families. The chapel was filled wall-to-wall with people. We had nowhere else to go, so we made the best of it.

Rules to Live By

Everyone who lived there had to keep their possessions outside in large storage lockers. All we brought from Mexico were two bags of clothing and a doll for me. But while at the shelter, we got head lice and were forced to throw out all our clothes and replace them with used stuff. I was so sad. We had to throw away these beautiful handmade dresses from Mexico. I'd always felt like Cinderella when I wore them.

Each day at 6 A.M., everyone was required to go to Bible reading. Then we went to our lockers and gathered what we needed for the day—clothes, toiletries, books. Next, we'd wait in a long line to take a shower, which was timed. Once, my mom accidentally went over the time limit and was humiliated when the staff came in to tell her she had to get out. And I really hated the ladies' room. It had one mirror, a sink and two doorless stalls, so there was no privacy!

At 8 A.M., we ate breakfast in the basement. I felt like a beggar, standing in that long line. When it got too noisy, the director flashed the lights in the dining room and said, "Stop serving!" until everyone quieted down. It made me feel so low, like we were nothing.

After school, I came straight home because dinner was at 4 P.M. If you missed it, you wouldn't eat. So I couldn't hang out with friends or do after-school activities. After dinner, we had to attend church service. If we didn't go to church, we couldn't live in the shelter. We weren't allowed to watch TV, but we could listen to religious radio stations. At night, we had to sleep on the pews in the chapel. It made me incredibly angry. I thought, "Why can't I just be like everyone else?" But I knew my mom was working hard cleaning houses, trying to save enough for a place of our own. The least I could do was understand.

My friends had no idea I lived in a shelter. I was too ashamed of being homeless, so I told them I didn't have a phone and that my mom didn't allow guests. Girls would say, "Your mom is so mean!" That hurt because she's the nicest person, but I couldn't say anything to protect her. I felt terrible lying, but I felt even worse telling the truth.

My mom knew it was hard for my brother and me. She reminded us that there are places where kids didn't have half of what we had and told us, "There's nothing wrong with living in a shelter." It was so hard to believe sometimes.

Moving Out, Moving Up?

My mom cleaned houses so she could be with us after school. This was a sacrifice because she could have gotten a much better job. After three years in the shelter, a woman my mom worked for invited us to live with her. It was the most amazing thing, since we had nothing to offer in return. I'll always be grateful for how comfortable she made us. But my mom felt we were a burden, so we moved back to the shelter after a year.

When I was 10, my mom received government aid so we could get our own apartment. We could cook our own food, watch TV and live in a clean house! I was so happy!

Still, I couldn't escape my past. A boy who heard we'd moved from a shelter teased me, saying, "At least I never lived in a shelter!" I felt so terrible that I ran into the bathroom crying. My friend came in and asked, "Why would he say that?" I lied and told her I didn't know. I was too ashamed to tell her the truth.

A few months after we moved, my dad came from Mexico to live with us. But it wasn't long before their relationship went bad, and we had to leave him—and our apartment. I was so upset, but there was nothing we could do.

My mom found a family who let us live with them in exchange for her babysitting their kids. But the six months we stayed there were awful. The family got angry if we ate too much, and they constantly yelled at us, "This is not your house!" It was like we weren't even human beings.

'Fessing Up

Once again, we moved back to the Bible Tabernacle. I was 12, and the shelter had changed. It was cleaner, and we shared an apartment with other families so we didn't have to sleep in the chapel.

By then, I had become best friends with a girl at school named Emily [not her real name]. She was the easiest person to talk to, and we got along really well. She was my first best friend, probably because I'd never trusted anyone as much as I trusted her. Even so, I was too embarrassed to tell Emily where I lived, so I lied to her.

My conscience never stopped bugging me so, after a year, I decided to tell Emily everything. Since we didn't have a phone, I wrote her a letter saying, "The real reason you haven't been able to come over is because I live in a shelter, and it's so embarrassing to me." It was such a relief to tell her the truth, but I was afraid she wouldn't like me anymore. A few days later, Emily wrote back, "I will always be your best friend. Living in a shelter is nothing to be ashamed of. You should have told me!" I cried because I was so happy.

Emily asked if she could spend the night, and I was so excited! I couldn't believe anyone would want to stay with me in a homeless shelter! We had the greatest time, playing and dancing with all the other kids there. It was the first time I felt like a normal kid.

Life Is So Unfair

As hard as it was as a little girl, being a teen in the shelter was even harder. It was still really strict. I couldn't hang out with friends, join clubs, play sports or be a cheerleader because of my curfew. I thought life was so unfair but, deep down, I was grateful because I knew that, when it was cold, I had warm food, clothes and a roof over my head.

Still, some people are really mean. It hurt when strangers saw us get off the Bible Tabernacle bus and pitied us, saying, "Oh, you poor thing." I'd think, "Please don't treat me any differently."

When I was 14, Emily moved away. It was so sad, and we decided we'd be pen pals. But we lost touch with each other. I'll never forget Emily because she was the only person I ever trusted enough to tell the truth.

Home Sweet Home!

That same year, my mom saved enough money to rent an apartment again. Finally, we were really on our own—with a phone and no curfews! We're still here, and it's amazing. Even though we didn't have electricity at first, I was so happy, sleeping on the floor in my own room with the light coming in from outside my window. It was the most peaceful feeling in the world.

My mom works at a grocery store now. It's so much better because it's a steady job, and she gets great benefits, like health insurance. My brother is doing well and is growing up to be, well, a normal teenage brat! Actually, he's a good kid and never gets in any trouble.

Since I've always had good grades, I received financial aid and will attend community college this fall. I hope to become a social worker so I can help other homeless kids. It's hard for kids to understand what's happening, and I would love to make it easier for them.

Even though it was tough, being homeless has made me more understanding of others and really appreciative of what I do have. My friends complain about little things when they should be so grateful! My mom always says in her prayers, "Although we've been through a lot and don't have much, we have each other." Family is the most important thing you can have—even more important than having a home.

CHAPTER 2

Lessons Learned
from Running Away

You Win Some, You Lose Some, but You Live

William Dominguez

The following narrative was written by William Dominguez and appeared in L.A. Youth, an independent newspaper written by and for teens in Los Angeles, California. The newspaper, with a readership of about 400,000, was created to give student journalists a place to practice their skills and investigate serious issues facing young people without the threat of censorship that school-sponsored student newspapers sometimes face.

As Dominguez reports, he has had a challenging life. His father was physically abusive, and Dominguez avoided coming home even as a young child. He spent several years in foster care, but began running away and using drugs. After a while, Dominguez says, he was living in MacArthur Park in Los Angeles, sleeping on the playground equipment or under a bridge, and begging for money. He joined a "crew," somewhat like a gang, got into fights, and continued to struggle with his living situation. For more than a year he was in a locked-down group home, and at eighteen he was moved to what is called "transitional housing." Here, as he tells it, he began to make plans for a more stable future, and to believe that he could have a normal life. As his story ends, he thinks about becoming a roofer.

Shortly after writing this story in 2005, Dominguez left transitional housing without telling the staff where he planned to go. There is no record of where he is now, or whether he has a home.

Maybe you have seen those smelly homeless guys asking for money. But did you ever stop to think that one of them might actually be a teenager? I spent a year and nine

William Dominguez, "My Life on the Streets," *L.A. Youth*, May–June 2005, pp. 20–21. Reproduced by permission.

months on the streets. What I saw and experienced, no teenager should have to go through.

I grew up in an abusive family. When I was a little kid, I would stay out as long as I could around my neighborhood and at the park to avoid getting beat by my dad. When I was 5, my dad burned me on the stove and I was put into foster care.

I spent eight years in one foster home in the San Fernando Valley. I liked it. It was actually a normal family. We had dinner together. But I'd still get sick of it sometimes because I was the middle child and would get blamed for everything. I also got into fights with my foster parents over stupid things like my room being clean or homework. Sometimes I would run away for weeks and go to a friend's house. I was used to running away. The streets were like my home.

But when I was 13, I was taken out of my foster home. Social workers said there wasn't enough food or clothes and supposedly my foster dad was beating my little brother and sisters. I was sad to leave and surprised because I didn't think those things were true. I was placed in a group home where I lived with five other foster youth.

Going to a group home after spending so long in one place was hard. I didn't like how the group home staff didn't care when I told them I was getting picked on by the other kids because I was the new kid in the house.

I was in three group homes over the next month but from each one I went AWOL, Absent Without Leave. I would hang out on the streets by myself until I got stopped by police for being out past curfew. The cops would bring me back to the group home, but the staff wouldn't take me back.

Running Away Was My First Instinct

Then I was placed at a group home in Pasadena. It was cool because the staff listened to my problems. I stayed there for a year until I got caught with weed. They said they were going to kick me out. I thought that was unfair because it was nothing big. It was only weed. I was mad so I went upstairs, packed my bag and left. I took the bus to my friend's house in downtown L.A. As always, I didn't know how long I was going to be on my own.

I liked it at first. The freedom, drugs and everything were freakin' great. My friend's mom told me I had to get a job to help with rent. I tried to get a fast-food job or anything I could get. I filled out applications and asked if they had openings. But no one wanted to hire a kid with no education and who was a runaway. So after a few months, my friend's mom kicked me out.

I went to MacArthur Park near downtown. It was cold and smelled really bad. There were a lot of drug addicts and jumpings. I'd make friends and they would be like, "You wanna get high?" I started doing crack cocaine and other drugs like crystal meth, coke and speed. I had never used those drugs before, but when I was on drugs, I didn't worry about falling asleep, getting caught or eating.

When I wasn't high I would go to the library and go to sleep far away in the corner. Sometimes on Sundays I would go to the park and play basketball.

At night I would sleep in the jungle gym, in the slide that was a tube, because it was warmer. When it rained I would sleep under the freeway bridge. Once in a while I could get a good night's sleep. But other nights I couldn't because I was worried about getting caught by the police. Every now and then I would hear gunfire and it would keep me up at night.

My clothes were dirty and ripped. I smelled like piss and body odor. I would eat out of garbage cans or steal food. Before I started living on the streets I was a good 135 pounds. I lost a lot of weight. I looked like a twig. I would go a few days without eating. For the first couple days I would be starving, but on the third day the hunger went away and I couldn't feel anything.

"Can I Borrow a Dollar?"

I had to beg for money. I would ask for 50 cents or a dollar. I'd say, "Can I borrow a dollar so I can catch the bus?" I asked guys with their wives or girlfriends because they were more likely to help a kid out. Some people would look at me and say, "What a waste" or "Get the hell away from me, you bum." The ones who felt sorry for me would give me money and say "Poor kid." On a good day, I made $40 to $60. I'd go get something to eat. Then I'd buy drugs, alcohol and cigarettes with the rest of it. I smoked a lot of cigarettes and crystal meth. Drugs were more important than food. That's how it is for addicts.

It was scary at times. One time I was hanging out with this guy who had done a stupid drug deal. Later, we were sitting on a park bench and the guy he'd ripped off came back and started shooting at us. I ducked and fell to the ground. It was an adrenaline rush. I saw my life flash before my eyes. Luckily, we didn't get hurt.

While I was homeless, I thought of myself as nothing. I had no feelings whatsoever. I couldn't see myself still alive because of all the drugs I was doing, all the stuff I was seeing, all the people I was ripping off. I was breaking into houses and robbing them. I was afraid I would get caught. I thought I would overdose or get killed. Seeing little kids with their families was hard. I wished I had a family of my own.

I don't remember exactly when or how old I was, but I moved to the San Fernando Valley because it was familiar. I also had friends from middle school there. Once or twice a week I would shower or get something to eat at a friend's house. I made sure to go to different friends' houses so they wouldn't find out I was homeless. I'd tell them, "No one's at my house and I don't have a key."

My best friend got me into a crew. A crew is like a gang but you can get out when you want and they do smaller crimes like tagging. Being in the crew meant a lot to me. They were like family. They gave me food, a place to take a shower and sometimes a place to sleep. I would sometimes tag with them. They gave me the name AWOL after I told them how I ran away.

Picked Up by the Police

But one day I was asleep at a park and the cops came by. They saw me and ran my name through the police computer. I came up as a runaway so they took me in. I was mad because I was used to staying on the streets and living on my own. I had been on the streets for a year. I didn't want to go back to a group home.

After that, I was in and out of 13 group homes. I'd run away or get kicked out for having dirty drug tests. Each time I left I thought, "Here we go again." I would stay on the streets for one or two months, sleeping in parks or churches, then I would turn myself in. I don't remember much about this time because I don't want to and my memory is messed up.

I do remember that I went back to my crew for help. But they turned their backs on me. They said they weren't going to help me because I had lied to them about God knows what. But my best friend from the crew, Tommy, knew I hadn't lied so he let me stay with him. But I felt like I was interfering with his life. I was wearing his clothes and eating his food. I felt bad, so I left and was all alone again.

One night I woke up in the middle of the night crying, wishing I had a family to go to. I regretted leaving Tommy's house. I thought about selling myself for food and money, but I didn't.

The Breaking Point

I hit a breaking point when I was at a party with Tommy. I got in a fight and some guy came behind me and stabbed me in the side. That was it. I called my social worker and got the number for a runaway shelter in Hollywood. I stayed there for two months. I went to Narcotics Anonymous to get help with my drug problem, went to therapy and got my stab wound healed.

Then I was put in a foster home in Pacoima near San Fernando. But my rival crew was in the area. I got into fights and got threats every day. They'd say, "I'm gonna kill you. Get the hell out of this neighborhood." My foster mom didn't do a thing about it. So I ran away from there, too.

I felt really jacked up in the head when I realized I was going to be on the streets again. I was really scared that I would go back to my old ways of drugs and alcohol. After spending so long on the streets I felt like I had lost my mind. I had been stabbed. I had been shot at. I had seen people get shot and die or die from an overdose. I was tired of it. I started stealing and cutting myself and trying to overdose. I wanted to get caught. I wanted to die.

After just a week, I got picked up by the cops one night because I was falling asleep in a shopping center in West Hills. They asked, "What are those marks on your arms?" I told them I was feeling suicidal so they took me to the hospital. I was happy because I had food, a shower every day and a warm bed to sleep in.

Because of my running away and drug history, I was sent to a locked-down group home in Culver City called Vista Del Mar. I stayed there for more than a year. Sometimes I would act like I was back on the streets. I wouldn't sleep or eat for a few days and sometimes I did drugs. I still get the cravings to do drugs, but I've stayed clean.

Finally, Someone Believed in Me

One time when I was 18 they pissed me off to the point where I just walked out the front door. One of the staff stopped me by the gate. But they didn't kick me out. I don't know why. I guess they saw something in me. They said, "William, we know what you're going through. We're going to work with you." I guess they knew I was frustrated. I was 18 in a locked-up facility with no family, no freedom. They thought I was a good person. Holy crap. That made me feel weird. If they had kicked me out, I would have been on the streets for good.

A few months later I graduated from Vista. When I found out I was going to transitional housing, which is where older foster youth live, I had nightmares where I was back on the streets. I had been a screwup my whole life. I was worried that I'd screw up and get kicked out.

In transitional living I get more freedom. I can go out for 24 hours on the weekend and spend the night at a friend's house. It's still hard because I'm not used to having a roof over my head, being able to eat three square meals a day and having people that care about me, like the staff and my friends. I still sometimes want to AWOL but I don't. I'm older and wiser. I know I have no place to go to.

For the first time, I have plans for the future. I want to go to a trade school to learn roofing. I also want to get my own place soon. Then I'll have all the freedom I want. I know I won't return to drugs. I don't want to end up like my biological father in prison.

Like they say in the movie *Friday*, "You win some, you lose some, but you live. You live to fight another day." My past is part of me. It will follow me wherever I go, but hopefully it will be put in the past. Sometimes I don't regret living on the streets because it made me wiser. I know what I have to do to survive. I'm going to get a job and be somebody.

I'm Out Here for a Reason

Noreen Shanahan

According to the Canadian government more than fifty thousand Canadian teenagers are classified as runaways in a typical year. In the following narrative, Nicole describes the hard lessons she learned during her years as a runaway living on the streets of Toronto, Canada's biggest city.

Nicole ran away from home when she was fifteen, and got a ride to Toronto with her older boyfriend, Mike. As she relates, she had been beaten repeatedly by her stepfather, and she was on probation from an earlier charge; she believed that living with Mike would be a step toward a better life. For three years they lived on Mike's welfare checks and on what they could raise by panhandling, and Nicole reports that begging for money actually helped her gain confidence talking with strangers.

Unlike many of her friends, Nicole says, she never worked as a prostitute, but she did fall into a drug habit and found herself spending all of her money on Ecstasy. Finally, she says, she decided shortly after her eighteenth birthday that she should change her life. With the help of Toronto's Evergreen Centre for Street Youth and an alternative learning center called Beat the Street, she stopped using drugs and started taking classes to improve her job skills. Looking back, Nicole realizes that she made some mistakes, but refuses to wallow in guilt or self-pity; she simply wants to move on with her life.

Noreen Shanahan is a freelance journalist and poet, and a community activist in Toronto, Ontario, Canada. She also teaches a course in writing autobiography. She interviewed Nicole for a special issue of New Internationalist *magazine.*

Noreen Shanahan, "Nicole: 'I'm Out Here For a Reason; I'm Not Regretting It Any More,'" *New Internationalist*, April 2005, pp. 20–22. Copyright 2005 *New Internationalist* Magazine. Reproduced by permission.

I grew up in a small town. My mom and dad split up when my sister was just a baby. When I was a kid, money was tight. I don't remember my mom having a job. She used to volunteer at our school—stuff like that. For clothes we would go to shelters or second-hand stores. It was a rough time. But my mom and I were close. I remember saying: "I don't want to get old and if I do, I'm not going to leave you."

School was fun 'til they tried to change me. I was 13 then and when you're 13 you start doing your own thing and finding out who you are. I was dressing in baggy clothes and getting into trouble at school. My mom had just met my stepdad. He didn't like me and used to beat me up. He'd say that I was going to get myself into something that I couldn't get out of. He was the mess that I couldn't get out of! Once he banged my head again and again on the table. I told my real dad about it but he pretty much said it's my stepdad's house and he can do what he wants. It was his word against mine. I felt like I was on my own and I had to take care of myself.

My stepdad kept saying that all my friends were stealing so I must be stealing too. Then I went out and did a stupid thing. I became a tag-along in an auto theft. That was the first and last time I got into trouble with the police. My mom and stepdad came to the police station and said: "She can stay in jail and learn a lesson." After that it was: "You're going to a foster home. We're gonna send you away to these places for good." My stepdad said: "They will beat you and rape you at a foster home and you won't be able to do anything about it."

Leaving Home

I ran away in July 2002. I didn't pack a bag or anything. I took only a purse with cigarettes in it. That was all. I stole $40 [Canadian dollars, US $32] from my mom and we spent it on beer that night. I hung out in backyards and in the forest by our town and waited three days for my ride to the city. When I was hungry, I went to my friends' house when their parents were out and stole some food. The police were looking for me because I was on probation. But I figured if I didn't run away, I would've done something stupid or been sent away. When I got to Toronto, I called my probation officer and said I'd run away because of the situation. She agreed because my dad had called her and told her that my stepdad was beating me, and that's the reason why I got arrested. If you get hit you should tell someone—you shouldn't put it off.

My boyfriend Mike gave me a ride to Toronto. I was 15 when I ran away, and Mike was 23. My parents didn't know about him. In Toronto we crashed at Mike's friend's house for three weeks. Every day it was just walking around and stuff, and sleeping a lot. It was summer so it wasn't that bad. I found out that they play free music outside City Hall, so sometimes I just went there and listened. I didn't get on welfare for five, maybe six months. And it was hard to get on it because I wasn't 18, the regular age. They couldn't understand why I'd be 15 and run away from home.

It was two years before I saw my mom again. Mike was on welfare. At first the only money I got was from him. I wasn't worried about what to do the next day or where to sleep because at least I was out of a situation that I wanted to be out of. I had no clothes except for this thin pair of pyjama bottoms and a tank top that I wore for almost a month. I don't remember eating much and I lost a lot of weight. During the first five months food banks were my best friends. I don't think I'll ever forget the pain of hunger.

I stopped being shy when I was panhandling. People talked to me and I talked back. Some people would have conversations with me about dropping out of school and why I was on the street. One lady took me to Burger King for food. Once I had to fight for my corner of the street. A guy using a walking frame was yelling at me: "You're taking all my money," so another guy who washed windows told him to leave me alone, that I was a girl.

While I was panhandling, Mike sat in Coffee Time—in the smoking area—watching me. I didn't know he was there until once he came out because somebody was talking to me for a long time. I met some people on the street who were just watching me. This one guy got off the streetcar and said: "I live over there. Do you want me to watch you?" He would just come out every once in a while, see how I was doing, and on the days I had no money he gave me some change. I said to him: "There's nothing that you need to give me. Just watch me and make sure nothing happens. Like, if the police come, tell them: 'She's done nothing wrong.'"

When I first came to Toronto I met a girl who was just getting out of prostitution. I learned from what she told me. She was going through a lot. Many girls told me how hard it is to get out. If you get into the wrong group then maybe you can't, but if you don't then you're pretty much dead.

Cold Cash

If you meet a girl on the street and she's into prostitution, if she's not trying to get out then she's gonna try and pull you in. I thought about it plenty of times. In 10 minutes I can have 50 bucks. But it's 10 minutes of torture, pretty much, because who wants to do that?

Even though it's hard for me to trust guys, I don't really feel threatened by them. If I'm in a room by myself and they're flipping out, then I'm terrified. But if I'm on the street, and I know there's other people around, and I get confronted by a guy, I'm one hundred per cent—I'm like a bitch. I'll stand up to them no matter what and I'll threaten to hit them. And if they hit me I'll go after them because I've been through crap that I don't want to happen again.

What I think is particularly wrong is how the police don't treat prostitutes the same when it comes to rape. Rape is rape and everybody—no matter who: even if they were willing [at first] and then they changed their mind and said no—they should still be treated the same. And I know. I've talked to these girls.

When it comes to panhandling, us girls might get more money, because people won't question us as much on [things like]: "Oh is it going straight to drugs?" and stuff. But then people will say: "I'll give you a hundred dollars if you spend a couple of hours with me [for sex]." People just assume more from us. They just think we're something totally different.

There's always that one drug that will pull you in. For me it was ecstasy. It helped relieve me of stress. Makes you happy. Forget about your problems. I was hooked for a couple of months. All my money went straight to that. What's really, really hard is coming down from it the next day.

When I had a good binge on it and came down I was the biggest bitch alive. Coming down you feel really weak because when you're high you don't eat or drink water, so you feel dehydrated. When you come down you think about everything again and remember why you took it in the first place.

Lessons Learned

I stopped partying and started getting clean after my 18th birthday in July. The main thing I've learned since getting clean is that I need my education. It took me two years to go back to school. Even though here at Beat the Street [literacy upgrading for street youth] you don't get credits or anything, it's still working towards what I want to learn about. I've wanted to be a chef since I was a little kid. I just love working with food; I like to be creative with plates, giving a meal more colour—things like that.

My choice to be with Mike was an opportunity to get out of the situation at home. And afterwards, we just grew together. He helps me a lot and I was helping him with his problems at the time. He had an addiction, so when I first got with him he was just getting clean. He's been clean for the whole time we've been together and that's going on almost three years. So I guess I was his ground support.

If it wasn't for Mike I wouldn't have gotten in to the training programme, because I was pretty much depressed and didn't want to do anything. You get to the point that you don't even want to get out of bed. He kept telling me about his situation and what he went through and what he didn't do. Just knowing his mistakes ahead of time meant I didn't have to go through all of them myself.

I was feeling guilty for a while after I ran away from home until I spoke with my stepdad. He was like: "Oh this is what you wanted and now this is what you get." Once I heard that, I thought: "Well, I don't really care." I'll admit, if my stepdad wasn't there, I'd still be at home. But I'm out here for a reason. I'm not regretting it any more.

I learn from my mistakes. We all know what we have to do to help ourselves. And we need to find the strength inside to ask for help. Go to anyone you trust. Talk about it.

Not the Right Choice

Ernesto

The following narrative was originally published on a Web site called Runaway Lives: Personal Stories and Reflections by Runaways and Their Families. *The Web site was created by Judith K. Sandt, reference librarian at Pennsylvania State University at Lehigh Valley, as a way to put a human face on the statistics about teenagers who run away from home. Runaways and their families are invited to post their stories and reflections on the site—anonymously, if they prefer.*

In the essay that follows, a young man named Ernesto explains the sequence of events that led to his separation from his girlfriend and the child they have together. According to Ernesto, he was planning to run away in violation of his parole when he learned his girlfriend was pregnant. He ran away for a while, and while he was gone she had a miscarriage. He turned himself in and served time in jail, but maintained his relationship with his girlfriend. When her family turned against him, he writes, the couple decided to run away.

For four months they lived in Ohio, and Ernesto struggled to support them with a low-paying job. When his girlfriend became pregnant again she chose to return home, and her parents prevented Ernesto from seeing her. As he writes this narrative, Ernesto is living in another city, unable to see his son. He warns other teens that running away is not the answer to their problems.

Ernesto was born around 1983, and ran away with his girlfriend at the age of seventeen.

This is sort of a long story. It all started off with this girl I met about 5 or 6 years ago. I won't say her name, but on Aug. 15th of 2000 we started seeing each other.

Ernesto, "To My Baby Joey," *Runaway Lives*, November 7, 2002. Reproduced by permission.

It was all good. Her family liked me and every thing. It was like my second home. I loved it. I was on parole when we started going out. Things went kind of fast and in 4 months she was pregnant. I was already tired of parole so I skipped it one day.

The day I had decided to go on the run, I called her. That was the same day she had made up her mind to tell me. She asked me to come to her house because she needed to talk to me. I said Ok.

So I went. She told me that she was pregnant. That had ruined my plans for running away. . . . her mother had told me that if I wanted to have anything to do with my girl or the baby that I had to turn myself in. It took me awhile and while I was still on the run she had a miscarriage. . . . It hurt me a lot because I wasn't allowed to see her while I was on the run, so I couldn't comfort her.

Well, I talked to my mom a few days later and I told her that I wanted her to set up a plan so that I could turn my self in and to talk to my girlfriend's mom into letting me see her minutes before I had to go back to jail. All went as planned. I seen her for about one hour before my parole officer came to pick me up . . . it was the hardest thing I had ever done in my life . . . knowing where I was going . . . but I did it all for love. . . .

I spent almost 4 months in jail. She waited for me.

Her Family Turns Against Me

By the time I got out her parents were kind of iffy about me, but they were still willing to give me anouther [*sic*] shot. Her oldest brother wasn't though. He blamed the miscarriage on me. He said that I put too much stress on her, and it was crazy because me and her brother (we will call him Jay) ended up getting into it over a lighter.

See I wasn't allowed to go over her house when she was home alone like before so one day I had to go and get her mom from her grandma's house (her whole family loved me). Well, while I was at Grandma's I asked her mom for a cigarette and she told me to get it (it was in her purse). So I did, and when finally got to my girls [*sic*] house about a half hour later her brothers got home. Jay kind of gave me a dirty look. The other one was sort of a fallower [*sic*] so he didn't really do much. . . .

Then came the question "Ernesto, where is my lighter? You [were] the last one to use it?"

I replyed [*sic*] "Its [*sic*] in your purse, isn't it?" She said no. So I got up and with "trust" went through her purse. . . . Jay didn't really like that. . . . He started cursing and calling me names. . . . I didn't say anything so I wouldn't lose any respect for her mom, but my girl started laughing after Jay left. It looked like we [were] both laughing to her other brother so he got mad and the next day he told Jay since they work together.

Jay came the next day mad we got in to [*sic*] it and right after my girl said, sell your car and let's go tonight because they are never going to let me see you again. I said, ok, and in 2 hours I sold my car "cheap" got us 2 bus tickets . . . came back 4 [*sic*] her that same night. Everybody had left—Dad at work, Mom at the bar, Jay went home to his family out west, and her brother that was supposed to be watching her went over her cousins' house. . . . she was home alone.

On the Run

So I went for her that night. We spent two days in the city I'm from and then took off to Ohio. We spent about four months on the run.

At first it was pretty cool. A friend helped us get fake IDs and everything. I got a job after a few days, and after I got enough money, we got help and we got a apartment in about a month. It was hard. Fun had turned into hell. She didn't work and, I mean, I was only 18 and I had bills to pay, rent was due, I had to buy food. I was supporting 2 of us with a 7 dollar job. Then she got pregnant again—now that was a experience I'll never forget.

We waited for about 3 months, then she wanted to go home. So we waited for a little bit and I bought a car (a real crap mobile) and we came back leaving practically everything I had worked for.

Everything didn't go quite as planned. The car broke down like 3 hours away from our destination. A trucker ended up helping us and gave us a ride back to the city. When I took her back home on X-mas eve I went to AZ [Arizona] for about 1 week then went back to my city to try to see her, but her mom had put a restraining order on me so that I could not see her. But still I saw my son be born on July 22, 2002 on my b-day. I was the happyiest [*sic*] man alive.

But even after I held my son Cruzito I messed up . . . doing drugs and all kinds of stuff. I had to move to another city to change my life and I am. . . .

Running Away Is Not the Answer

My thoughts and advice for all you teens out there—running away doesn't solve anything. I've done it more then once before this story. It only puts a hold on your problems and sometimes makes them bigger. Look, like I said my son was born July 22 of this year, and it's now November 6th and I haven't seen my son in almost 3 and a half months and I miss him. . . . I miss him with all my heart. But I keep running and that is why he is not here with me right now. I ran for too long, then finally they turned their backs on me. They stopped trying and I have lost my first baby boy forever.

So please stop [while] you are ahead. . . . and if you're like me you won't realize what you have untill you have lost it . . .. then it's too late.

To my baby joey

My Son Is Repeating My Mistakes

Blazesmom

The narrative that follows was originally a posting on a Web site called the Nineline Forum, *an online message board sponsored by Covenant House. In addition to a twenty-four-hour hotline that teens can call if they are having trouble with family, relationships, abuse, drugs, or other problems, Covenant House provides the forum as a space for teens and their families and friends to express their thoughts about their conflicts.*

The following essay was written by a woman who calls herself "Blazesmom." According to the author she had an unhappy childhood herself, and left home at seventeen to escape an unloving mother. For a time she lived on welfare, traveled with a carnival, and roomed with a fifteen-year-old prostitute. When she became pregnant with a son, Blaze, she decided to try to straighten out her life.

As she explains, she had two more children within a few years. She tried and failed to form a close relationship with her mother. She married a man who turned out to be abusive to the children, and then married another man who she says is gentle and loving, and a good provider. However, just as she seemed to be reaching stability for her family, fifteen-year-old Blaze ran away from home.

The author shares her anger and confusion with her son's decision to run away. She asks teens who may be reading her essay to post replies online, advising her how to respond to Blaze's refusal to come home.

When i was a teenager, my mom wasn't very nice to me. i wanted to commit suicide when i was 9yrs old but i found a LOT of comfort in writing. i won't give the details.

Blazesmom, "I'm Blaze's Mom," *The Nineline Forum*, April 29, 2007. Reproduced by permission.

but it's typical. alcoholic mother who used to get beat all the time, makes the right choice, leaves abuse behind, leaves alcohol behind but doesn't seem to change as a person, as a mother. she didn't know how to take care of me but she did take care of my older brother. she fed me, somewhat clothed me. but she didn't do so well at loving me. so when i was 14, i decided this was all stupid. i was tired of being the kid she raised. i tried to be someone else but she wouldn't let me. she wanted someone like i used to be, the scared kid that did what she told me to. i couldn't be that anymore. when i was 17, i quit school and decided to leave home. she had no problem with it at first. i guess she thought i would come back. i didn't. when me being gone started to affect her social assistance, then she got very mad. and she got mean. i didn't talk to her for five years. she never called the police or Child and Family Services.

i moved in with my abusive and controlling boyfriend. i got on welfare. i traveled with the carnival. i moved across the country and was "found" by a distant aunt. when i was 18, i moved back to my home town. i made new friends, met up with old ones. i partied hard. i got broke really fast. my friend and i were going to become prostitutes but i ended up pregnant. and i didn't know who the father was—one of four or five guy friends i had. my friend was a run away, 15yrs old. her mother never called the police or Child and Family Services. she did become a prostitute, was raped and became a drug addict. i was her bouncer on the street and would stand on her corner, big and pregnant, protecting her. i never knew she had a drug problem, even though we were room mates. i didn't drink and i didn't do drugs. i was always a "good girl" even when i was partying. i never smoked.

i had a son named blaze. as soon as i got pregnant for him, i knew i had to stop living on the street. my friend used her money from hooking to take care of me while i was pregnant. then when blaze was born, she and i took care of him together. for a little while. i knew living with a hooker just wasn't a good idea anymore. i ran away from my best friend. i moved a lot when blaze was a baby, i changed apartments or houses every year for the first seven years. i had two more children. and even though i became friends with my mother again, it didn't last. she just isn't the kind of person i wanted to know. and she also chose to leave and go live with my brother across the country, even though i felt my little family really needed her. but my mother never lived with me for more than five years straight.

Married, but Not Happy

i got married and i thought it was a good thing. i left university and became a stay at home mother with a truck driver husband who had two university degrees already. we moved to a different city almost ten hours from my home town. i didn't know anyone. i homeschooled my children. and my husband was not happy. neither was i. so i left him. me and the three kids moved back onto welfare, back into government housing. no matter what tough times i had, i always had my kids. i never gave them up, never left them. i wasn't always a good parent, but i was learning fast what to do and what not to do. i tried really hard.

when blaze turned ten years old, i cried. i was so happy! someone in my life had spent a full ten years with me. i felt i must not be so bad after all. i must be an alright person after all.

i got back with my husband after a few years. and i had a fourth baby, but not before finding out how abusive my husband was to my other children. i fought for custody of my fourth child and kept him. i keep my ex husband as far from my family as possible, even though i have to share custody of the baby with him. i'm married to the right man now, the kind that never yells, never hits, never drinks. the kind of guy who was willing to move across the country just to be with me—because that's what he did. and everything was so good for the last two years. we were not on welfare, we made our own money. we always did our best to make sure all the kids had what we could give them. we don't have lots of money, but we have lots of love.

Blaze Runs Away

blaze ran away on monday april 23, 2007. he is 15yrs old. i called the police and got Child and Family Services [CFS] involved. and i don't know what to do. every brochure, every pamphlet says not to go drag him home. but every instinct inside me says THIS is where he belongs! he didn't leave because he was beaten. and he didn't leave because we are mean. he left because he didn't like the rules. because i said no, you can't be out EVERY night. no, you can't hang out with the people YOU told me were drinking and doing drugs. no, you can't have access to the internet EVERY day.

i just cry and cry. CFS knows where he is but they won't tell me. there is no protection issue here, he hasn't told them he's been abused or anything. everyone keeps saying he'll come home. but to me, it's like he's died. it's like he went away and i don't get to have a funeral and i don't get to say good bye. he doesn't want to talk to me. he doesn't want to see me.

he's not going to run to the streets and do drugs. he's not going to start drinking. he's with a good family, that CFS at least trusts. but he's not with me, where he should be.

he says he doesn't feel like he fits with my family. but how can that be truth when without him, i feel like my family is torn apart and shattered?

i want to call the police and have them get him when he starts going to school. but i told the CFS worker to tell him i would not pursue him there. that would break his trust. and if the police drag him home, he will just run away again.

i don't know why the family he is with thinks its okay to not encourage him to come home. i don't know why they think his decision is the right one. i'm very angry with them.

A Mother's Questions

i'm angry with blaze. why does he think this is the right thing to do? what is he trying to say? am i so bad of a mother? i was never mean, i never called him names, i stopped spanking when he was 3yrs old. and i tell ALL my kids that i love them, every day. he doesn't want hugs, what 15yr old tough guy kid lets you hug them? i have hugged him anyway.

we didn't have an argument. the day before he ran, it was earth day. we had a picnic in the park, the kids played hide and seek in the trees and we took turns flying a kite. we bought ice cream, big ones.

i found out after going through his email that he thinks he loves this new girl. but he loved the one he had last month too. and he loved the girl before that. is all of this because of a girl??

every resource tells me "he will come back". but they didn't know him. i knew him since i was only 18. i know him second best, only HE knows himself better than i do. and he's stubborn and smart. if he's got more stuff with this other family, and they're treating him like he's the victim of some horrible controlling mother, he will never come back. he will not see that i was fair to him, he will not see that i was keeping him safe. i was not too hard on him. i was careful, involved and i talked to him, soo soooo much. i always involved him in decisions and did make the final choice but only if i had to as the adult. i didn't rule his life. i never checked his email until after he ran away, never snooped in his room. so whatever he is thinking, to me it looks like a story he's concocted so he can keep being with people who will give him everything i couldn't.

what do i do? i want to know what teens think about this. because this kid, he's the one that defined me. he saved me from badness, time and time again. his existence made me a better person. to have him so gone from my life, who am i without him? who am i if i am not blaze's mom?? why is this happening? i'm not an alcoholic, i'm not a beater, a hitter. and i'm not rich and keeping everything for myself. i really love him. i really do! why did my son leave?

i don't know if this story will be posted by the admins or not. i hope it is. because i wish teens could tell me what to do. what THEY think i should do. the education packages and professionals say to just wait it out. but i ran away too. and i didn't go back, not ever. i want my son back! how do i show him that i don't accept his decision to run away, without betraying his trust?

Supporting My Sister's Decision to Leave

Carl Holm as told to Liz Welch

Teenagers run away for different reasons, many having to do with uncomfortable family situations that the teens do not know how to resolve. In the following narrative Carl Holm discusses his family's religious belief in polygamy, or marriages with one husband and two or more wives, and how the practice of polygamy led both him and his sister to leave the family.

According to Holm he received a phone call from his mother saying that his sixteen-year-old sister Fawn had run away from home. Holm contacted Fawn, and learned that she feared being forced into marriage at a young age, as two of her cousins had been. He says that he decided he would support Fawn's decision to leave home, and would fight to be named her legal guardian.

Holm reflects on his own childhood in a family with an abusive father, two mothers, and eighteen siblings. He says that he used drugs and alcohol at an early age, and married his wife Joni when he was only seventeen so he could leave his father's home. Decades later, he writes that he is determined to save Fawn from the same struggles, although he acknowledges that he might be facing a long court battle and further rejection from his parents.

Liz Welch, who interviewed Holm for this narrative, is a freelance journalist whose work has been published in several magazines including New York, Real Simple, Glamour, *the* New York Times Magazine, *and* Inc.com.

I got a call from my mother one Sunday evening in January, which was odd, because she never calls. There was panic in her voice. She said: "Fawn has run away. If she shows up on your doorstep, please take her in." Fawn is 16 and my youngest sister. I said, "You bet I will."

The funny thing is I hardly know Fawn. I'm 40 and happily married with four daughters, 15 to 22, but the moment I heard she'd run away, I felt a twang in my gut, because two decades ago I left my family, too, and never looked back. The next evening, my wife was watching the news, and there was Fawn with Flora Jessop, a children's advocate who rescues girls from polygamy. I spoke with Fawn soon after. She told me that she didn't want to go back home because she thought she'd be married by 18. At least two of my nieces were married at 14 and now have children, so the fear was real. I decided at that moment I'd fight tooth and nail to get custody of Fawn.

The first time I knew my family was different was when I woke up one morning and saw a strange purse on our kitchen table. That's when my mother told me I had another mother who was going to live with us, too. I was 7. My parents are Fundamentalist Church of Jesus Christ Latter-day Saints, a faction that broke off from the Mormon Church when worshipers in Salt Lake City officially renounced polygamy.

We moved to Salt Lake City when I was nearly 8. My dad tried to keep me and my siblings isolated from other kids and what he called their "evil influences," but we all went to public school, so it was hard. Once, I begged my dad to go roller skating. He said no, but I sneaked out anyway. He showed up at the rink, chased me down a back alley and beat the tar out of me. My father believed that the things kids enjoy, like roller skating and baseball, were a waste of time—I should have been home reading Scripture or doing chores. I was the oldest son. He'd call me out in front of my siblings to set an example.

By the time I was 13, I had started drinking and taking drugs. I did it to impress my friends, but more so to rebel against my father, who would inevitably find out and then beat me. A year earlier, I begged the Division of Child and Family Service [DCFS] to help me get away. Instead I was put in a foster home for about three weeks while my father and I attended counseling together. When DCFS told me I had to return home, I was devastated. I wasn't sure how I'd survive. At the time, I had 18 siblings and we lived in a six-bedroom house. But by that point, my dad had forbidden my siblings to hang out with me.

When I was 16, I met my wife, Joni, at Salt Lake Donut, where I was working. Several months later, I asked her to marry me. I loved her, but I also wanted to get out of my father's house. Since I was only 17, I had to get permission. My parents weren't willing at first, but then they consulted their spiritual leader, who was, at the time, my great-grandfather Leroy Sunderland Johnson. He said, "Don't let these kids live in sin!" I was elated, but then only my mom and one sister came to my wedding. Being shunned by my family was harder than I imagined. Though my marriage emancipated me, Fawn's would enslave her. I had to do something to help.

Facing Our Parents in Court

Flora Jessop had arranged for Fawn to stay at a safe house in Phoenix. The first few times we spoke, she was very cautious. All she knew about me was what my family told her—that I was supposedly covered in tattoos and consumed with self-loathing. Still, Fawn told me that she asked my mother if she could come live with me before she ran away. Despite my bad reputation, I was still a beacon of hope for her.

In mid-January, I went to Arizona to accompany Fawn to her first assessment meeting with representatives from Child Protective Services [CPS] and other agencies. She told them that she didn't want to return home. (By then, my family had moved to Arizona.) Fawn said she wanted to go back to school; she hadn't been since fifth grade. One of my daughters is a year younger than Fawn, and her biggest concern is whether she will be a writer, an architect or a pop singer. I had to hold myself back from taking Fawn home with me right then and there.

Federal law says that Arizona's CPS has to make reasonable efforts to reunite parents with their children, unless there is a safety concern. I've heard of cases in which girls who ran away from their families because they were worried about being forcibly married wound up being returned home. Next thing you hear, they're married, pregnant and trapped.

In late January, my mom called again, and I asked her point-blank to give me custody of Fawn. She refused. The next time I saw my parents was a few days later at a dependency pretrial hearing. I knew they would be angry. They came expecting to take Fawn home, not to see me. I'll have to face my parents in court again in July, which I'm not looking forward to. But it's worth it if the state places Fawn with me. My sister wants to live with me, but she doesn't realize what this means—that her family will ostracize her, or how terribly painful that is. At least I can offer her a touchstone. I can say, I know what it feels like.

SOCIAL ISSUES
FIRSTHAND

CHAPTER 3

Trying to Help
Teens in Trouble

Trying to Do the Right Thing

Martha Tod Dudman

When they have found that their own discipline has not worked to keep troubled teenagers from what they see as dangerous behaviors, many parents have turned to private schools and counseling centers that promise to help young people with "tough love," or guided, intentional strictness. In the following narrative, Martha Tod Dudman describes her conflicting emotions after she had her runaway daughter, Augusta, placed in a residential private school for troubled teens, and how difficult it was to feel connected to her daughter when their only contact was through letters and long-distance phone calls.

From the time Augusta turned fifteen, her mother says, she was angry and self-destructive, using drugs, running away from home, dropping out of school. Dudman, a single mother who had had a troubled adolescence herself, had done everything she could to protect her daughter and son from the difficulties she had faced. As she watched Augusta spiral out of control, she could not help but blame herself for failing as a parent.

Before the beginning of the following excerpt from her memoir, Augusta, Gone, Dudman reports that Augusta had been sent to Forest Ridge, an expensive residential school in Oregon, far from the family's home in Maine. Augusta felt that she was being rejected by her mother, while Dudman felt that she could not help her daughter survive without professional help. Just before the excerpt begins, Augusta has run away from Forest Ridge, and been brought back. In the section that follows, the author explains that Augusta had to prove to the staff at her school that she was ready to return, and that much of Augusta's anger turned on her mother. As Dudman remembers a few difficult weeks, she reveals her own feelings of love and fear and anger.

Martha Tod Dudman was president and general manager of Dudman Communications, a group of radio stations, during the 1990s when the events in Augusta, Gone *occurred. She is also the author of a novel, and of* Expecting to Fly *(2004), a memoir about her own teen years.*

FROM MY HOTEL ROOM in rainy Seattle I speak to the woman at the "safe house" where Augusta's staying for $350 a night. They will take her to the program the next day (transport, $325). None of it has any meaning. I've already FedExed the check. I finally ask if I can speak to her but they say no, not now, it's better if you don't.

"She's fine," the woman tells me. "She's watching television."

So instead I speak compulsively to everybody connected with her in any way—to the parents of the other girl. To the man who took her there. To the people at the Wilderness Program. I tell them to watch out. That the last time she was there she cut her wrists. Don't give her a knife, I tell them. Watch her, I say. I want to talk to everyone. I want to go there and put my arms around her. I want to go there and keep everyone off her. I want to hug her. I don't want to see her. I don't even know if I know her. I don't even know if she's sane.

And I don't get to speak to her for three weeks.

I do write her a letter, which they assure me she will get to read during her "solo" on the desert.

Sitting in my office home in Maine. I write: I'm so glad you're safe.

She writes me back an angry letter, which they fax to me. "I'm always safe," she tells me. "I can take care of myself."

There is one phone call and she just yells.

The school isn't sure they want her back. I have to talk them into it. Is it because I'm not paying full tuition or do they know something I don't know?

They say they think maybe she ought to be somewhere else. Somewhere, they say, "restricted." Like a jail?

All the time I'm at work. We're negotiating the sale of the radio stations, but nobody knows about it and it might not even happen, so I'm still planning the New Year's Eve dance party at the Ellsworth Holiday Inn. I'm hiring a disgruntled ex-salesperson who worked here years ago, then worked for somebody else, now might come back. She wants way too much money.

But I have this little edge when I'm negotiating all these things. I don't care. They tell you, when you're learning about business, that you shouldn't care too much. But I *really* don't care. Three million. Four million. So what. Four hundred. Six hundred. Fine. I don't care who pays for the paper tablecloths that will be soggy with cheap spilled champagne fifteen minutes into the new year. They pay. We pay. Okay with me. I'm winning everything. It's amazing. I should have done this years ago. Had cancer.

Augusta's at the Wilderness camp for three weeks this time. I'm on the phone with the Head of the School trying to talk her into taking Augusta back. I'm on the phone with my education consultant, who says she'll talk to the school. I'm on the phone with [Augusta's counselor] Rose, who is inexplicably scrubbing pots noisily the whole time we're talking, and I imagine her in a battered West Coast kitchen in some funky hippie seventies abode in her big skirt scrubbing away while we talk. She sighs and says, still scrubbing, that she'll fight to get Augusta back in.

"I specialize in tough cases," she tells me. "I'll go get her myself, if I have to," she says.

I want to trust her, I want to think that she will save Augusta, this enormous woman, but I don't know if she's really gifted, a wonderful counselor, a magician, a sage, or just some lumpy weird one with no life. She's all I've got. She's the one who tells me she can save my daughter.

I speak with Augusta's "field supervisor" in the Wilderness, who tells me one week that Augusta is "really negative," "not buying in," "furious," "self-pitying." The works. But the next week she says that Augusta has had a really good week, is being a leader, helping other kids. I grab at this one.

"That's how she is," I tell this woman I will never meet, somewhere in Idaho. "She's really compassionate. She's very charismatic."

I don't know if she's charismatic. I don't know if she's crazy. They're hinting that she might be crazy. I don't know.

One night Nina's mother calls from California. She's the girl Augusta ran away with. Nina's staying home, her mother tells me.

"You would not believe the things they did to her at that school."

The mother tells me that they scream at the kids. That they told Nina she was a slut. She asks if I would like to speak with Nina.

Nina gets on the phone. Her voice is light and high. I try to picture her. I only met her once. She looked so tiny. Dark eyed. Dangerous. Disturbed. But on the phone she sounds only young.

"No, I'm not going back there," she tells me in her little voice. "I'm doing really good."

I tell her I hope she takes good care. I pretend I'm talking to my own daughter who will not talk to me.

The school says they don't want her. They want her in a lockup. That's what they do. If Forest Ridge doesn't work. There's always someplace else.

But then the Head has a phone call with Augusta and Augusta says she's ready to go back. That she'll try harder. That she'll be good.

So they relent after the three weeks and she goes back. We have our first conference call together and I am supposed to tell her how I felt when she was missing, with Ben [Augusta's father and the author's ex-husband] and some stupid staff counselor who doesn't know the right things to say. Who has been told what to say but keeps getting it wrong. Rose is on vacation. So we get this one instead. This lummox. We want Rose. She knows what to say.

"So," he says, the way they teach them, "tell Augusta how it was for you when she was missing."

I go first because Ben always makes me go first.

But it's not the way Rose does it, and we're all uneasy and I get it wrong and sound too harsh telling her how sad and scared I was; how I thought she was dead. How I cried, how sad Daddy was. I tell her about walking up Schoolhouse Ledge and saying her eulogy, about telling her friends, about how it was for us when she was gone.

Augusta cries and says she doesn't care. She says we kicked her out, that we don't care about her. She says we didn't write to her. She says she didn't call because she didn't want to get caught. She says she has dreadlocks and she has to get her hair cut. Her voice gets higher and she starts speaking faster. She's going to run away again first chance she gets. She wanted to cut her wrists again when she was in the car being escorted back from Wilderness to Forest Ridge. She would have cut her wrists, but she didn't have a knife, she says. She would have. She doesn't want to talk anymore. She hates us. She wants to go home.

They're watching her, they assure us. Watching her.

One of the kids is assigned to follow her around. The staff will keep their eye on her. She's safe.

I'll go out in December and see her at the next parent seminar. If she's still there.

I might sell the stations quicker than I think. Then what? What will I do then?

I want to feel normal again.

I want to just be in my house and go on a hike and go home and read on my bed in the late afternoon and have the children there with me, young again, when they still loved me. Was it ever like that? Some Hallmark card of a life? I don't remember.

I want to get rid of stuff. Out of Augusta's room. My own junk. My desk. The books that I don't read. The bathroom towels.

Anything I don't use or need. Get rid of it! Old clothes! Boxes of stuff! Letters from college! Get it out.

I want to be free to move around!

I came here with only a knapsack and a typewriter twenty-four years ago.

And look at all I've accumulated—a house! piles of clothing! two children! an ex-husband! books! boxes of letters! dishes! tiny shampoos from fancy hotels! vases! canned goods! jewelry! computers! acres of old journals! couches! bedsteads! toys galore! stuffed animals! and heaps of memories like wet rags, bunches of them, hanging off me, weighing me down.

I want to rise up, weightless and triumphant. I want to move unencumbered. The walking. The running. The escape.

How come she gets to run away? I want to. I want to run away. Out of my house, out of my towering, choking stuff swallowing me up in its dusty maw. Out of my own skin even. Out of my life with its restrictions and regrets and resistance. I want to run away, too. I want to run away—directionless, hatless, coatless—without a bag or even the knapsack that I brought a quarter-century ago when I came here to Maine.

I am going to see her in December and Jack [Augusta's brother] is coming with me. Ben is going. We are all going. It turns out we are all going on the same plane—across the country all together, a ragged little band, her family.

I remember when she was younger, eight or nine, and we were having supper at the Colonel's Deli downtown, Augusta, Jack, and I. We used to go there often. I would bring whatever book we were reading and read to them quietly at the table while they drew on the paper place mats and we waited for our food. Pepperoni pizza. Cole slaw. Onion rings. Fish chowder. Grilled cheese sandwich. White bread and a pickle.

We liked it there. We went off-season—in the spring, when it had opened and it all felt new, and in the cold fall, when it stayed open after Labor Day and all the summer people had left except the old ones. We got a back booth and we read there and we had our meal. The little three of us.

This time Augusta had on her considering look. "I wish we were a normal family," she told us. "You know, a mother and a father and a sister and a brother. Maybe you should get married, Mommy."

"Marry who?" I asked.

Did she really want me to marry Thomas, my boyfriend then, with his shabby house, his odd poetic silences, his bony face?

"No, I guess not," she said. "And anyway, if you were married, then we'd have to wear those certain kind of hats. And I'd have to wear little dresses and Jack would have to wear a tie."

Always there was a hunger. Stronger than I realized. To be like other kids, or how she imagined other kids. Their normal lives. Their balanced families. Their TV dreams.

Augusta is not doing well at school. She is angry and surly, they tell me, and won't participate. Again, there is talk about not keeping her there—that she ought to go somewhere tougher, somewhere harder. In spite of all the evidence I keep wanting to believe it isn't really so bad. It can't be.

They say she feels as if nobody loves her.

Will she ever get better? I need to pray hard.

I have to balance everything. Not let anything show. Then at one early-morning Rotary board meeting in Bangor, I let it slip. I'm at a table with people who have become my friends, meeting here 7 A.M. month after month discussing the business of Rotary. This morning we are discussing one of our members who hasn't paid his dues. He's been sick, somebody says, maybe he just forgot.

But people have to pay their dues to stay in Rotary. He's had reminders.

Then I speak up. I can't believe I'm saying this. We're all eating blueberry muffins. And I say, "Maybe you don't know, but I've been through a pretty horrific year myself this year, and I forgot my Internet access payment. I always pay my bills right on time, sometimes early. But I just forgot about it."

I stop then, like that explains it, what I mean, but they all just stare at me like sheep.

Then I'm embarrassed. I'm almost crying. If someone had put their hand over my hand lying on the table just then, I would have cried, but instead they all look aside and talk about other things. They don't know what I'm talking about. They're embarrassed for me. This isn't, after all, a group therapy session. This is a board meeting. This is not the place.

I try to remember that, but sometimes, through this long year, I've tempted to just blurt it out. Tempted, at Rotary, when it's time for Happy and Sad Dollars, when people take turns getting up waving their dollar bills and announcing they're giving a Happy Dollar because their son graduated high school with high honors, but a Sad Dollar because he got into Colby (and guess who's paying!). Happy Dollar for their daughter's wedding. Happy Dollar for their seventh grand-child. Happy Dollar for their thirty-fifth wedding anniversary. I've thought about it, sometimes, then, standing up. Giving a Happy Dollar myself. My daughter is alive. Sad Dollar: they say she might be crazy. . . .

I'm getting Christmas presents to take out to her. A blue fuzzy sweater that I hope she'll like. A couple of books. A new journal. "You always give me a journal," she always says. We're going out to see Augusta.

But then something happens.

The phone's in Jack's room. The call comes in the middle of the night. I don't even hear the phone ring, or if I do, I hear it in my dream. I don't wake up until my son's standing in my bedroom door.

"It's the school. They're on the phone. They said it's an emergency."

He brings the phone in, hands me the receiver in the dark. I roll over on the bed and hold the phone up to my ear.

"Hello."

"Hello, it's Rebecca Mintz. I have to tell you something."

"Is Augusta okay?"

"Yes, Augusta's okay."

"Did she run away?"

"No, she's fine. She's here."

So now what? Tell me.

"We have had a difficult situation here," Rebecca goes on. "We're dealing with it. Aaron Golden has committed suicide. We just found his body this afternoon."

I don't care. My daughter is okay. My daughter is safe.

They were hardly friends, Rebecca tells me. He broke up with his girlfriend and then he disappeared and later they found his body hanging from a tree in the woods near the school. They are calling all the parents. All the kids are in a giant all-school group. Everyone is upset. But Augusta is all right.

I know this is a terrible thing. This is the worst thing that could happen to those other parents, but this is how you think when you get this way with your kid—that's all there is. All you care about is that your kid is all right. Everything else falls away. Everything else is burned away. There was a suicide and it is very sad of course but it is not my suicide and it is not my kid.

That's how it is. You know it's selfish, but you are unashamed of your desire for only your daughter. And you are unashamed of your uncaring. It doesn't matter. This one time your kid's okay. It's somebody else's.

We talk some more and she tells me Augusta will call me tomorrow and then we hang up.

Is Jack still awake?

I call into his room.

"Honey?"

He hardly answers me. And then I realize I haven't told him. "Augusta's okay," I tell him.

"You mean she's not dead?" he asks.

And I realize he has been waiting in his room, not knowing, waiting in the dark not knowing, scared for his sister in his room.

And I flash back to my son years and years ago lying in his bed sad, worried, he was such a worried boy! Unable to sleep lying in his bed when I used to come up the stairs and peer down the hall, long after he had gone to bed, long after he should have been asleep, and there he would be, lying on his side, facing the door, and I could see his eyes shining in the dark, watching out into the hall, waiting because he couldn't sleep but he didn't want to get in trouble, didn't want to call for me again.

"Yes, she's fine," I tell him, and I go into his room and I tell him about the other kid but he doesn't care really either. Augusta's okay. That's what we care about. This time we're okay too.

The day before we leave I sign the deal to sell the radio stations. I tell my people. Nobody is shocked. They all sort of knew anyway. Now there will come the bumbling-around part, everybody discussing it, looking at me weird. I'm glad I'm leaving.

We're all on the plane together—Ben, Jack, and I—and it's snowing hard and the plane's a nineteen-seater and icing up and they have to deice it and there's wind and it rocks through the stormy sky on the way to Rockland on the way to Boston and I think: What if we all go down? How would that be for Augusta? All her family.

She's not in good shape, they have warned me at the school.

It's a long way west to Oregon, especially when you're traveling with a fifteen-year-old boy with no room for his legs. Especially when you're traveling with your ex-husband and going to see your daughter, whom you haven't seen in three months and who, during that time, was missing for over a week. It's a long way even by plane, especially when the movie they show you is *Zorro* and all you have to read is old magazines and a book you thought you'd like but really don't.

We wind up late into Portland, missing the last plane out to Bend, so we rent a car and drive, the three of us. There's ice on the roads and our little car skids around. Ben drives and Jack sits up front, and I lie down in the backseat, where it's quiet.

It's dark out and my ex-husband is driving up and down the mountains of Oregon. I can feel the little car climb the windy roads. Up front I can hear them talking about cars and boats and other things, things that don't interest me too much. And I lie in the back, tired, curled under my down jacket, with the seat belt off. I can see the edge of the sky around the tops of their seats, and out the side window. A couple of far stars and the black night. Lights ripple through the car as trucks go by.

I can hear their voices talking quietly on and on about uninteresting things.

It feels like when I was a kid, riding in the backseat of my parents' car with them in the front talking to each other. I could hear their voices. I was tired. It was late. I could hear them talking about things that didn't interest me, but the sound of their voices was comforting. They sounded faraway. As if they were riding in another car, on another road, somewhere else.

I'd be half asleep lying like this in the back.

I can see a piece of the sky. I can feel the car rumbling over the road. I can hear their voices and the silences between their sentences and I feel safe. Safe enough to sleep.

I Was a Hired Thug
for Tough Love

Sheerly Avni

In the previous narrative, Martha Tod Dudman described her conflicting feelings of guilt and hope after she sent her daughter, Augusta, to a special residential program for troubled teenagers. In the following narrative Sheerly Avni describes her employment in one of those programs, leading the teens on wilderness trips, often against their will.

The program that Avni worked with for two years was a three-week therapeutic wilderness program. The teens who participated had been forced to attend by their desperate parents or by the courts. The hope was that after three weeks of strict discipline and carefully planned problem-solving, the students would be ready to resume their education, generally at a special boarding school.

Avni tells the story of Karen, a young woman who announced from the beginning that she would follow all the rules during her stay, but did not intend to change who she was. As soon as the program was over, she said, she would return to her boyfriend, who had once broken her arms. For days Karen silently did as she was asked, but she resisted any encouragement to analyze or discuss her own feelings, dismissing these attempts as "mind games." Finally, during a challenging ropes course, Karen had a breakthrough. Moments like this, Avni says, make up for any doubts she has about the value of forced treatment programs.

Sheerly Avni is a film and culture journalist based in San Francisco. At the time she wrote this narrative, she was an editor at The Beat Within, *a publication written by and for incarcer-*

Sheerly Avni, "I Was a Hired Thug for Tough Love," Salon.com, August 30, 2000. This article first appeared in Salon.com at http://www.salon.com. An online version remains in the Salon archives. Reprinted with permission.

ated young people in the Bay Area. She is a former editor of Salon.com, *and writes for various periodicals including* AlterNet *and* TruthDig.

"How the hell do you sleep at night, knowing what you did to kids?"

Twitch was a 16-year-old reporter at Pacific News Service [PNS]. He had come to us through juvenile hall. He'd lived on the streets, kicked drugs at a younger age than I'd ever done any and had the face and attitude of an arrogant 22-year-old. We were taking a cigarette break outside, and he had asked me what I'd done before coming to PNS. When I told him that I used to work for a therapeutic wilderness program, he froze for a second. "Wait, so this was one of those lockdown camps?"

"Yes," I said, preparing to launch into my Heartwarming Story of How Lost Souls Find Themselves in the Desert.

But I didn't have time. His eyes widened, his face broke open and for a second looked young and scared and hurt, and then it slammed shut. He asked me his question, threw down his cigarette and walked away.

It was a year before he could speak to me without glaring, and two before he would tell me why: When he was 13, he'd been escorted—kidnapped, he'd say—to a therapeutic boarding school similar in many ways to the program I used to work for. The school had since been closed down and he was suing for abuse.

So how do I sleep at night?

The Goals of the Program

For two years, during all seasons, I led wilderness trips for teenagers who didn't want to be there, who had been begged, cajoled, bribed, tricked and sometimes physically dragged from their beds before getting dropped in our laps. Once they arrived, their clothes were taken and their piercings pulled, and their Walkmen, cigarettes and makeup were put into storage. Then they were dumped into the custody of two assholes who showed them how to roll up tarp and webbing and a sleeping bag into a pack, marched them into camp and told them that from now on they'd need to inform one of us every time they wanted to go to the bathroom.

As one of the assholes in question, I offered very few answers, even fewer expressions of sympathy, and had little information to provide them about why they were there or what they could expect. We would tell them that they'd discover for themselves what they needed here, and that our job was to teach them the skills they needed to survive and to keep themselves safe.

It was usually at least a week before any of them would stop thinking of me as "that bitch."

Their parents would spend the three weeks of the program planning for their kids' future with the help of an educational consultant. These consultants, often of dubious credentials, would help the parents decide what to do with their out-of-control, drug-using, sleeping-around, disrespectful, underachieving, overmedicated, underappreciated, blue-haired, multipierced, ADHD, ADD, OCD, dyslexic and usually damned unhappy kids.

In the end, the kids were often sent off to yet another kind of institution, generally referred to as "emotional growth schools." These schools often charged upward of $60,000 a year and promised all the happy endings we promised, except more of them and for longer.

And the same umbrella company that owned us also owned these schools.

Sometimes I felt as if I was only there to smooth the kids over, prep them and fatten them up for their next step. We may have been in the business of miracles, but business is still business. And healthy, balanced kids? That was our product.

But I didn't deal with parents or schools or experts or the people above the people above me. I was just out there with the kids and the canyons and the campfires. The miracles.

Like Karen.

Karen's Resistance

Karen showed up with 2-inch-long, fake purple fingernails set with rhinestones. According to routine, the outfitters had taken her clothes and given her the things that she would need for the trip—everything from a T-shirt and hiking boots to oatmeal and a pocketknife. She was small, with mascara-smudged tear stains under her eyes and long black hair that she braided and unbraided as I laid out the tarp and showed her how to roll it up into a bedroll over her sleeping bag and blanket. I introduced myself and my co-instructor, Rob, and then asked her how she'd ended up here.

Her eyes were flat. "Two f---ing goons woke me up in the middle of the night and put me on a plane."

I nodded, unrolled the pack I'd just put together and told her to try it. She stood up and looked me straight in the eye. "Look, I don't know what kind of Outward Bound bullshit this is. And I'll do whatever it takes to graduate and get out of here in 21 days. But if you or my parents or anyone else thinks that you're gonna change me or make me into a good little girl by sending me to boot camp, I'll tell you right now, it's not going to work."

I nodded again, and then went to talk to Rob about the fingernails. We had a hushed conversation. Would she be able to build traps, carve wood, build fires and tie complicated knots with those purple claws? Would we have to file them down? Would she get them caught in something?

We couldn't worry about it now. There were four other kids sitting on their packs 30 feet upstream, all in various stages of discomfort and unhappiness, and we had six miles to go by noon if we wanted to beat the midday heat.

Over the course of the next week, Karen was true to her word. She hiked five to 10 miles a day without complaining. She learned how to set up traps; she learned how to make a fire by striking a rock against her pocketknife; she learned how to build a shelter from plastic, string and branches. She did her journal assignments; she spoke when we asked her to, stayed quiet when we asked her to. And on Day 7, when the therapist drove out in an ATV to meet with her, Karen told her the same thing she told us: She wasn't buying into any of the bullshit or falling for any of the mind games.

By Day 9, the kids weren't expected to spend as much time alone. Now we worked together in a group, sat by the fire in a group and, yes, talked about our feelings in a group. Jason explained why it had been so hard for him to quit cocaine. Christie cried about her parents' divorce. Joey, who had been in and out of boarding schools and rehab for years, told funny stories about other therapeutic hiking trips he'd been on.

And Karen sat, quiet.

Lisa, the therapist, had instructed us by radio that we shouldn't push her—just leave her be and let her know we cared.

First Revelations

On the night of Day 9, Karen told us that her boyfriend had once broken her arms with a baseball bat. Her parents were trying to break them up by sending her away. But he'd changed, she said, and she was just following all of our rules so she could get this over with and go home to be with him.

We knew from her paperwork that there was more—an abortion, constant fights with her father, hanging out with a tough crowd. We also knew that she probably wouldn't be going home.

On Day 10, our supervisor drove out and told Karen that her parents had made a decision: When she graduated from the wilderness program, she would go straight to a private boarding school in Texas.

I went for a walk with her away from camp. She was crying and cursing, throwing rocks, clenching her nailed fists so hard I was afraid she'd cut herself. We knew that she no longer had a reason to follow any of the rules. But she had a role in the group: The other kids needed her and there were still places we had to go, wood to be collected, water to be filtered.

That night by the fire, Jason said, "You know, Karen, I'm not sayin' I'm glad your parents sent you away. But I will say this: If I ever see that guy of yours, I'm gonna kick his ass."

Karen wouldn't have heard it from us. But from Jason—17 years old, earnest and Southern, always the first to carry gear or go get water—it meant something real.

But she still wasn't going to fall for any bullshit games.

"I love him," she said. "And he's not like that anymore."

And she was pissed at her dad. When she'd gotten pregnant, he'd called her a slut and refused to take her to the clinic. He wasn't there for her then, and now he was going to take her away from the one person who loved her? She wasn't having it.

The Ropes Course

Two days later, we brought all the kids into base for a ropes course. It was lousy weather for a course: The heat made the helmets unbearable, and it was so windy that the ropes and poles shook. Karen and Joey were the first to go up. They climbed up a 40-foot pole and then crossed shaky parallel bars with nothing but each other to lean on as they made their way to the other side. Lisa, who was both my supervisor and the assigned therapist, was walking everyone through it, making every step they took into a metaphor.

You know how those metaphors work. Anyone who has ever had to go on a corporate bonding retreat or a scout trip has heard it all before: Climb a ladder and heal your soul.

But after you've spent two weeks hiking, cooking, and sleeping in the canyons, where there are no city lights and no distractions, and nowhere at all to hide from your demons, it's tough to be cynical. When you're up there, you're in it, you're hooked.

They'd completed the first leg when for no reason whatsoever Joey sat down on the platform, curled his arms and legs around the post and said, "I'm not moving." They had been about to embark on the second of three legs, the one you can't do alone. One person has to hold onto the post and support the other, who walks out on a wire, with nothing to grab but a hand, and then leaps for a rope, which takes the person over to the other side. Without Joey, it would be almost impossible for Karen to do.

When Joey shut down, Karen was already out on the wire, and without his hand, she was a good 3 feet from the rope she'd need to reach the halfway point of the course. She could turn around and climb down pretty easily though, and that's what we were expecting her to do.

But Lisa called up, "What are you going to do now, Karen?"

"I'm gonna f---ing jump is what I'm gonna f---ing do!"

"Why can't you do it alone, Karen?"

"F--- you!"

"I mean it. Look at him. He gave up on you. He wasn't there for you. So what are you going to do?"

Karen rained down another stream of curses at Lisa, who stood with her hands on her hips, squinting into the sun.

"You gave everything you had, and now you're alone. But you're not falling, you're standing straight and tall. What's next?"

Karen just sobbed. All of us—Lisa, Rob, the kids—stood riveted, waiting. "F--- you, Lisa! I know where you're going, and it's not going to work! I ain't buyin' your bullshit!"

"I didn't ask what you were going to *buy*, I asked what you were going to *do*. He left you, and you didn't fall. Do you want to give up, or do you want to want to keep going and see if you can make it on your own?"

I looked sharply at Lisa. It was my 10th trip, and I'd never seen anyone do this leg without a partner. She was breaking the cardinal rule: Never set up a kid for failure.

But Karen shouted, "I'm going to f---ing keep going."

We barely breathed as she shook and swayed in the wind 40 feet above us, and then finally started to take mincing steps on the rope, cursing like a fishwife the entire time. We couldn't see her face, just her body shaking against the gray sky. Minutes passed. And then, without notice, she sprang for the other side.

And made it.

One More Step

Down on the ground we started clapping. And Karen, predictably, yelled at us to shut the f--- up.

Lisa called up, "So now, before you swing down, I've got one more thing to add, OK?"

"What?"

"If there's anything you want to leave up there, if there's anything you don't want to take with you, you can leave it. OK?"

"F--- you. I told you I ain't buyin' this shit!"

But see, there was no requirement. She didn't have to finish the course to graduate, or to win a prize, or to win respect from a group of kids who already respected her anyway.

She took a deep breath and jumped. We all ran toward her, but she ran first to Lisa, who held her for a long, long time. And then we picked up our packs and headed back for the canyons in silence, single file.

That night by the fire, after rice and beans, after making ash cakes from flour, after telling stories, she stopped us as we were about to say goodnight. "Wait. I want to tell you guys something."

Jason fed the fire. Christie stopped whittling her bow drill. Tim just looked away.

She whispered, not to us, but to the flames in the center of the circle.

"I just want you to know, I left him up there."

Jason stood up and put an arm around her. She buried her head in his shoulder and started to cry.

"But I still ain't buyin' this shit."

Karen did get sent off to Texas. Maybe she hated the school. Maybe she has never forgiven her father. Maybe she's back with the arm breaker. Maybe her moment on the ropes course was just that, a moment.

But it made for one hell of a moment.

And that, Twitch, is why I sleep at night. Because out in the canyons, Karen was the rule, not the exception. And what she did up there had nothing to do with her parents, or fancy group therapeutics, or watered-down Native American camp-fire rituals, or the people who owned the people who owned us. It was just plain courage.

And she never even broke a nail.

Teens Need Self-Reflection, Not Lectures

Hector Gonzalez

In the narrative that follows, Hector Gonzalez, a youth gang mentor, explains why he thinks listening is the most important thing a mentor of troubled young people can do. Gonzalez reflects on an intervention program he attended, in which the presenter did most of the talking, and remembers how he had typically responded with indifference to that kind of program when he was young himself.

Gonzalez works as a youth mentor/gang intervention specialist with an organization called the Filipino Youth Coalition. The students he works with are affiliated with gangs, and many of them live in foster homes or in the streets. Shortly after he began this work, he discovered that his most powerful connections with young people occurred when they took the lead in group discussions, instead of listening to him lecturing or raising what he considered to be the most important discussion topics.

Gonzalez tells how he travels to schools and to young people's neighborhoods to get to know them in their own territory. He describes Peter, a high school student who is trying to avoid the mistakes his brother made, and a camping trip the author and his colleagues took with fourteen teenagers. He concludes that it is hands-on experiences and personal reflection, not lectures, that will help young people change their lives.

Hector Gonzalez is a commentator, a hip-hop artist, and a mentor in San Jose, California, where he grew up surrounded by gang culture. He writes for Silicon Valley De-Bug, *a Pacific News Service publication written and illustrated by young people in the Silicon Valley of California.*

Hector Gonzalez, "Why Gang Intervention Doesn't Work," *Silicon Valley De-Bug*, September 2, 2005. Reprinted with permission of John Wiley & Sons, Inc.

I attended a "gang intervention" workshop a few days back. Being that I work with young gang members myself I wanted to see how other people were approaching their work. A Latino male with tattoos addressed the classroom about gangs. It reminded me of when I was 13, when I was the youth listening to the Latino male with tattoos give his spiel about why gangs are bad. The program was a repetitive discussion that went around in circles.

The programs both then and now consisted of a Latino male with a beard that lectured why people joined gangs and the results of gang banging. They show pictures of dead gang members, pictures of gang tattoos, they talked about prison life, and then gave a compelling story of how they changed their lives. What I have come to realize is that people don't change by reflecting on the lives of others, they change by reflecting on themselves.

At the age of 18, not to long after I had graduated high school, I was offered a position as a tutor for an organization called Filipino Youth Coalition (FYC). One month into my job, one of my co-workers gave up his position as a Youth Mentor/Gang Intervention Specialist and the position was offered to me. When I first began, I was lost—a young adult that gave lectures to kids from a curriculum that even I found boring. I realized that if there was anything that was profound, it wasn't in the workbooks, but in the relationship that I was building with the students.

A New Approach: Listening

Ever since that first job, I have worked in the middle schools throughout the East Side of San Jose. When I returned for my second year of the program, one of the students from the prior year came to the after school program and told me that she wanted to come in but that she was now in a foster home and that she would have to ask her social worker to let her stay after school. I walked with the student to the front of the school to talk to her social worker, and she explained to me that it was part of her foster home's policy to be home by a certain time, and that participating in an after school program wouldn't allow her to come home on time. As these words came out of her mouth, tears began flowing down the student's cheeks. I understood my job in a much different form after this point. I realized that people's testimonies of their lives were much more profound then any lecture I could ever give.

Many times, people that do gang intervention say that people join gangs because they want belonging or because they want to fill a void. If that's the case, then young people should be given the opportunity to reflect on those voids and lack of belonging as opposed to having a discussion on how "gangs are not the answer." Besides, the only person that would know that is the person who feels empty and like they don't belong to anything.

The FYC gave me the opportunity to develop my own curriculum. The truth of the matter is that although I developed a curriculum, I didn't even follow it usually. Most of the time, the young people were the ones that lead the direction of the program, talking about what they felt and telling me their life stories. I touched the general topics that the program and school required me to touch, such as drug prevention, peers, identity, family and academics. But I would run my program by creating a space where the students had an opportunity to identify themselves before I could identify them.

This was in some ways the opposite of the rest of the spaces they entered. Every other group, or institution that they belonged to identified them first. The school gave them an identity, they were either good or bad students, their teachers identified them as being trouble-makers, disruptive, and as low performing students. I asked them to tell me who they were, and they described themselves as strong young people, loyal to their family and friends, and they had dreams and goals.

For the past four years, I have devoted a good part of my life to working with youth throughout the eastside. Some of the most profound stories that I have ever heard have come from young people close to a decade year younger than I am. During a workshop with about 20 young people in a room and me as the only adult, a 13-year-old female shared the testimony of her life. She told the classroom that her health is dictated by her mother's drug problem, for when her mother was pregnant her mother abused methamphetamines. Her mother died not too long ago from an overdose. Her reflecting on this event is much stronger than any lecture I could ever give to her.

Hope for Peter and Other Kids

Although most of my work took place at the schools, it continued in the streets. I did home visits in hoods such A-town, Poco Way, and Verde to name a few. I hung out with them, met their OG's [original gangstas; members who have been around a long while] congregated as if I was one of their own. The last time I went to A-town, I drove by and parked my car in front of around 20 Cambodian youth most were in between 13–17 years of age all in blue, one guy was holding a Beebe gun, a couple of them were smoking cigarettes, I approached my little homie Peter. He shook my hand as his homie was riding his lowrider bike, the one I bought him for keeping his grades up and graduating 8th grade. Peter's older brother is currently locked up, and both Peter and his little sister recently completed their probation hours. His lips are very dark and he has scars on his face, his knuckles have scars on them as well, and he wears a tank top to display his home made tattoo that spells out his name.

I looked at his community. A-town stands for Avalani Town. Avalani is a street that contains apartments mostly occupied with Cambodian folks. In this particular visit to A-town I observed everything that my eyes captured; the kids running on the streets, all the A-town Crips lined up on the side walk, cars with busted tires, and apartment lawns with no grass, decorated by scattered liquor bottles. No matter how awful anyone thinks A-town is, it belongs to Peter, it is his and he takes pride in it. Peter lives gang culture, he doesn't need anyone to define it for him or tell him the consequences of gang banging, his family is living it. If Peter ever does decide to leave his gang, it would be through a realization that will manifest through analyzing his life and through self-discovery.

I realized that my role as a mentor was to provide a space for self-discovery, there is no setting better than a youth retreat outside of their hoods. Two weeks ago, along with some colleagues, I took 14 youth camping, three of them were females and the rest were males. They were all 8th graders. They came from all gang backgrounds, Norteno, Sureno, Cambodian and Laotian Crips. Half of the kids had criminal records, and most of them had been involved in a gang related fight at their school. Some of them had tattoos and all of them claimed to have a gang affiliation.

During the first day of the three day camp I asked them to introduce themselves by answering, "What is it that you fear?" With the exception of two kids, they all said that they feared their fathers. For the first time, they all shared an intimate moment with their "enemies." Throughout the camp we did activities that talked about our own strengths, families, and other discussion that dealt with us taking control of our destinies. For those three days they bonded; they played hide and seek together, ate together, laughed together, and shed tears together. The last night young Crips, Surenos, and Nortenos hugged one another.

Although they returned to their hoods represented by different gang sets, they will embrace the moment when with the help of their rival gang members, they were able to share some of the most symbolic moments of their lives, reflect on them, and heal their wounds.

After hearing the testimonies of so many kids, I know for a fact, that the only way to help anyone transform their life is by creating a space where people can have intimate moments by sharing their lives, reflecting on them, and finding the solution for their problems by themselves and for themselves.

Stick with Street Kids, No Matter What

Mark

In the essay that follows, Mark, a man who works with homeless and runaway teenagers, explains the importance of persistence.

Mark relates his history with a man named Tony, whom he met in 1981 when Tony was eighteen and already had a history of trouble. Although Mark and Tony came from different backgrounds and were of different races, they formed a bond in the short time Tony lived in the shelter where Mark worked.

Over the next seventeen years, Mark stayed in touch with Tony, who was in and out of prison on drug charges. When Tony finally got clean in 1998, he thanked Mark for his help straightening out his life. Mark concludes that one of the best ways to help troubled young people is to never give up on them.

Mark lives and works with teenagers in Essex, Vermont.

I work with homeless and runaway teenagers. I am still puzzled how I ended up in this field. I was a business major in college, but after two years of making money on Madison Avenue I left it in order to devote myself to helping kids get off of the streets, away from drugs, crime and gangs. Twenty-six years later, I am still at it. All I can say is that God led me here.

When you are working with street kids, I believe one of the most important things is that you stick with them, no matter what. One of the first kids I met, back in 1981, was Tony. African-American, from a single parent family in Harlem, he had spent most of his childhood in foster homes and group homes, finally aging out of that system at 18 and hitting the streets. We had zero in common but for some reason

Mark, "This I Believe," thisibelieve.org. Reproduced by permission.

that didn't matter. We found a bond. He only lasted in the shelter I was working at for two months. He was kicked out for coming in high on angel dust one night and tearing up the place. I'd see him out in Times Square every once in a while for the next few months, handing out flyers for some porn theatre, trying to convince passers-by to come in. Then he disappeared.

Four years later I was chatting with a prison chaplain I knew, and Tony's name came up. The priest had seen him recently in the main New York City jail, Riker's Island. He told me no one ever visited Tony.

So I went to see him. Tony was stunned to see me. He gave me a big hug and we talked for an hour. He was in there for selling drugs, and he expected to soon be shipped upstate where he'd spend the next few years. I gave him my address and told him to write, promising that I'd do the same.

"I Never Stopped Writing"

He was sent upstate, he did write and we corresponded regularly. Eventually he was released, but re-arrested on another drug charge. This cycle continued for a good dozen years. I never stopped writing, nor did he.

By 1998 he stopped getting arrested and one day called me to invite me to come to a Narcotics Anonymous meeting in the city. "It's my one year anniversary of being clean," he told me. I went. It was an incredible moment. When it was his turn to speak, he pointed to me and told the crowd, "See that white guy over there? (I was the only Caucasian.) I wouldn't be alive today if not for him."

We live in different parts of the country now, but to this day I talk to Tony by phone at least once a month. I am the godfather to his little girl, who is now age 8. He works, lives in an apartment and in a few months celebrates ten years of sobriety.

I'm glad I hung in there with him.

Organizations to Contact

The editors have compiled the following list of organizations concerned with the issues debated in this book. The descriptions are derived from materials provided by the organizations. All have publications or information available for interested readers. The list was compiled on the date of publication of the present volume; the information provided here may change. Be aware that many organizations take several weeks or longer to respond to inquiries, so allow as much time as possible.

Beat the Street
35 Jackes Avenue, Toronto, Ontario
M4T 1E2
Canada
(800) 555-6523 • fax: 416-323-3522
e-mail: information@frontiercollege.ca
Web site: www.beat-the-street.org

Beat the Street is a literacy program of Frontier College for out-of-school youth between the ages of 16 and 29 who are at-risk, street-involved or homeless. The concept that began Beat the Street came from Rick Parsons and Tracey LeQuyere, who knew from their own experience that poor literacy skills are one of the most common barriers to being able to access jobs, housing, services, and an improved quality of life. The Web site includes a link to a magazine called *Runaway Train*, writing and photos by street-involved youth at Beat the Street.

Child Welfare League of America (CWLA)
2345 Crystal Drive, Suite 250, Arlington, VA   22202
(703) 412-2400 • fax: (703) 412-2401
Web site: www.cwla.org

CWLA is an association of nearly 800 public and private non-profit agencies that assist more than 3.5 million abused and neglected children and their families each year with a range of services. The League also works through advocacy and education to shape public policy regarding the welfare of children, and conducts research to determine and disseminate best practices for professionals and volunteers working with children. The Web site offers press releases, research results, and descriptions of programs.

Children of the Night

14530 Sylvan Street, Van Nuys, California 91411
(818) 908-4474 • fax: (818) 908-1468
Web site: www.childrenofthenight.org

Children of the Night is a private organization founded in 1979. It is dedicated to assisting children between the ages of 11 and 17 who are forced to prostitute on the streets for food to eat and a place to sleep. The group works with detectives, FBI agents, and prosecutors in cities including Los Angeles, Hollywood, Las Vegas, Seattle, Miami, New York, Minneapolis, Atlanta, Phoenix, Hawaii, and Washington, D.C., and provides a twenty-four-hour-a-day hotline staffed by trained staff who can help teens find shelter, counseling, and protection.

Covenant House

Times Square Station, New York, NY 10108-0900
hotline: (800) 999-9999
www.nineline.org
Web site: www.covenanthouse.org

Covenant House is the largest privately funded nonprofit agency in North and Central America providing shelter and other services to homeless, runaway and throwaway youth. Its "Nineline" crisis hotline, at 1-800-999-9999, takes free and confidential phone calls from young people, while an online service at www.nineline.org allows young people to post questions and participate in forums and blogs. Incorporated in New York City in 1972, Covenant House International has facilities in 21 cities throughout the United States, Canada, Guatemala, Honduras, Mexico, and Nicaragua. Its Web site offers information for prospective advocates and volunteers, and a link to its newsletter, *The Covenant House Beacon*.

Family and Youth Services Bureau
U.S. Department of Health and Human Services
Washington, DC 20013
(202) 205-8102 • fax: (202) 260-9333
Web site: www.acf.hhs.gov/programs/fysb/

The mission of the Family and Youth Services Bureau (FYSB) is to provide national leadership on youth and family issues. FYSB's services focus on reducing risks by strengthening families and communities and helping all youth to thrive. Target populations include runaway and homeless youth, victims of family violence, children of prisoners, and youth at risk for early sexual activity. The Web site features posters, brochures, fact sheets, research reports, and links to other agencies.

National Center for Missing and Exploited Children (NCMEC)
Charles B. Wang International Children's Building
Alexandria, Virginia 22314-3175
(703) 274-3900 • fax: 703-274-2200
Web site: www.ncmec.org

Created in 1984, NCMEC is a private nonprofit agency working in cooperation with the U.S. Justice Department to help prevent child abduction and sexual exploitation; help find missing children; and assist child victims of abduction and sexual exploitation, their families, and the professionals who serve them. The agency maintains a twenty-four-hour crisis hotline, and a CyberTipline for reporting suspected child victimization. The Web site features news reports, statistics, testimony, videos, and advice for parents, attorneys, and others.

National Clearinghouse on Families and Youth (NCFY)
PO Box 13505, Silver Spring, MD 20911-3505
(301) 608-8098 • fax: (301) 608-8721
e-mail: info@ncfy.com
Web site: www.ncfy.com

The National Clearinghouse on Families and Youth (NCFY) is a free information service for communities, organizations, and individuals interested in developing new and effective strategies for supporting young people and their families. The Family and Youth Services Bureau (FYSB), U.S. Department of Health and Human Services, established NCFY to link those interested in youth issues with the resources they need to better serve young people, families, and communities. The organization has a library of free and low-cost publications on youth issues; a searchable database with abstracts of thousands of other documents; youth development resources; and a free monthly electronic newsletter.

National Runaway Switchboard
3080 N. Lincoln Ave., Chicago, IL   60657
(773) 880-9860 • fax: (773) 929-5150
e-mail: info@nrscrisisline.org
Web site: www.1800runaway.org

The National Runaway Switchboard maintains a twenty-four-hour-a-day crisis hotline at 1-800-RUNAWAY, which teens may call if they are planning to run away, if they are worried about a friend who has run away, or if they would like help making arrangements to return home. Funded in part through the U.S. Department of Health and Human Services, the organization provides nonjudgmental support to keep young people safe. The Web site offers articles and advice for teens and parents, a newsletter, and other educational materials.

National Safe Place
2411 Bowman Avenue, Louisville, KY   40217
(502) 635-3660 or (888) 290-7233 • fax: 502-635-3678
Web site: www.nationalsafeplace.org

Safe Place is a national youth outreach program that educates thousands of young people every year about the dangers of running away or trying to resolve difficult, threatening situations on their own. It provides access to immediate help and supportive resources for all young people in crisis through a network of sites sustained by qualified agencies, trained volunteers and businesses. Cooperating agencies display the yellow Safe Place logo, so that young people in trouble can identify places where they may walk in and obtain help. The Web site provides fact sheets, newsletters, reports, and statistics.

National Student Campaign Against Hunger and Homelessness
National Organizing Office:, Chicago, IL 60605
(800) NO-HUNGR • fax: (312) 275-7150
e-mail: info@studentsagainsthunger.org
Web site: www.studentsagainsthunger.org

Founded in 1985 by state Public Interest Research Groups (PIRGs), the campaign is committed to ending hunger and homelessness in America by educating, engaging, and training high school and college students to directly meet individuals' immediate needs while advocating for long-term systemic solutions. In the 2005–2006 academic year, 465 high schools and colleges were active participants. The organization offers training materials, information about hunger and homelessness, and opportunities for volunteers.

RunawayTeens.org
500 NE 1st Avenue, Miami, FL 33132
(786) 499-7798 • fax: (786) 425-1079
e-mail: info@runawayteens.org
Web site: www.runawayteens.org

RunawayTeens.org is an educational Web site sponsored by Kidsearch Network, a nonprofit organization that helps police find missing and abducted children. For teens, the Web site describes the dangers (including drugs and prostitution) they might face if they leave home. Adults will find warning signs that a child is considering leaving home, and advice for restoring solid family relationships so that a child will not want to leave. Also includes statistical information and a teen blog.

StandUp for Kids
1510 Front Street, San Diego, CA 92101
(800) 365-4KID • fax: (888)453-1647

e-mail: contact@standupforkids.org
Web site: www.standupforkids.org

The mission of StandUp for Kids, an independent organization founded in 1990, is to help homeless and street people aged twenty-one and younger. Volunteers in twenty-nine states, Washington, D.C., and Mexico identify, befriend and support young people living in the streets, and work with schools and through the Internet to help young people find ways to stay off the street. The Web site provides short videos, statistical information, and a link to subscribe to the *StandUp for Kids* monthly newsletter.

For Further Reading

Books

Sue Books, *Invisible Children in the Society and Its Schools.* Mahwah, NJ: Erlbaum, 2007.

Andy Butcher, *Street Children: The Tragedy and Challenge of the World's Millions of Modern-Day Oliver Twists.* Carlisle, UK: Authentic Media, 2003.

Rene Denfeld, *All God's Children: Inside the Dark and Violent World of Street Families.* New York: PublicAffairs, 2007.

Marni Finkelstein, *With No Direction Home: Homeless Youth on the Road and in the Streets.* Belmont, CA: Wadsworth, 2004.

R. Barri Flowers, *Runaway Kids and Teenage Prostitution: America's Lost, Abandoned, and Sexually Exploited Children.* Westport, CT: Praeger, 2001.

Claire Fontaine and Mia Fontaine, *Comeback: A Mother and Daughter's Journey Through Hell and Back.* New York: ReganBooks, 2006.

Kief Hilsberry, *War Boy: A Novel.* London: Picador, 2001.

Jeff Karabanow, *Being Young and Homeless: Understanding How Youth Enter and Exit Street Life.* New York: Peter Lang, 2004.

Katherine E. Krohn, *Everything You Need to Know about Living on Your Own.* New York: Rosen, 2000.

Jerry E. Lindsay, *Chain Gangs and Castles: A Runaway Teenager's Odyssey.* Authorhouse, 2003.

Marjorie Mayers, *Street Kids and Streetscapes: Panhandling, Politics and Prophecies.* New York: Peter Lang, 2001.

John Hagan and Bill McCarthy, *Mean Streets: Youth Crime and Homelessness.* New York: Cambridge University Press, 1997.

Roslyn Arlin Mickelson, *Children on the Streets of the Americas: Globalization, Homelessness and Education in the United States, Brazil, and Cuba.* London: Routledge, 2000.

Lynn E. Ponton, *The Romance of Risk: Why Teenagers Do the Things They Do.* Basic, 1998.

Renee C. Rebman, *Runaway Teens.* Berkeley Heights, NJ: Enslow, 2001.

Laurie Schaffner, *Teenage Runaways: Broken Hearts and "Bad Attitudes."* Binghamton, NY: Haworth, 1999.

Natasha Slesnick, *Our Runaway and Homeless Youth: A Guide to Understanding.* Westport, CT: Praeger, 2004.

Karen M. Staller, *Runaways: How the Sixties Counterculture Shaped Today's Practices and Policies.* New York: Columbia University Press, 2006.

Clare Tattersall, *Drugs, Runaways, and Teen Prostitution.* New York: Rosen, 1998.

Wendelin Van Draanen, *Runaway.* New York: Knopf, 2006.

Judy Westwater and Wanda Carter, *Street Kid.* New York: Harper Element, 2006.

Les B. Whitbeck and Dan R. Hoyt, *Nowhere to Grow: Homeless and Runaway Adolescents and Their Families.* New York: Aldine de Grutyer, 1999.

Periodicals

Dean Alford, "A Throwaway Generation," *Christianity Today,* April 24, 2000.

Ann Aviles and Christine Helfrich, "Life Skill Service Needs: Perspectives of Homeless Youth," *Journal of Youth and Adolescence*, August 2004.

Lutaa Badamkhand, "Dolgion: Life Is Given Only Once," *New Internationalist*, April 2005.

"Band on the Run: Troubled Youth," *Economist*, July 6, 2002.

Nicolas Barnard, "Runaways Flee Step-Families," *Times Educational Supplement*, November 2, 2001.

Arnon Bar-On, "So What's So Wrong with Being a Street Child?" *Child & Youth Care Forum*, June 1998.

Herbert R. Bennett, Jr., "Speaking Out for Homeless Kids," *New York Times Upfront*, November 28, 2005.

Charmion Browne, "When Shelter Feels Like a Prison: Memories of a Homeless Childhood," *New York Times*, August 18, 2002.

Popi Buchanan, "Life as a Runaway: How I Survived on the Streets," *Teen*, August 1998.

M. Gar Caswell, "Homeless for the Holidays," *L.A. Youth*, January–February 2001.

Kira Cochrane, "Our Young Runaways," *New Statesman*, April 3, 2006.

Shanda Deziel and Brenda Branswell, "The Anguish of the Street: There Are Thousands of Runaway Kids across Canada," *Maclean's*, August 23, 1999.

Shimon E. Einat, Spiro Rachel, and Peled Dekel, "Shelters for Houseless Youth: A Follow-Up Evaluation," *Journal of Adolescence*, April 2003.

Alicia Gallegos, "Ways Sought to Stop, Help Runaways," *South Bend Tribune (Indiana)*, December 6, 2006.

"Getting Tough with Troubled Girls," *U.S. News & World Report*, May 14, 2001.

Heather Hammer, "Vanishing Youngsters: No Easy Answers," *USA Today Magazine*, September 2003.

Mary Hampshire, "Somewhere to Call Their Home," *Times Educational Supplement*, December 15, 2000.

Florence Isaacs, "Mean Streets: What Makes Good Kids Run Away from Home?" *Parents Magazine*, September 1997.

Jim Jewell, "Children Huddled in Crevices," *Christianity Today*, January 2005.

Jason Kirby, "Extreme Measures," *Maclean's*, January 15, 2007.

Jennifer Leonard, "Anyone Could Be Homeless: A Girl Who Has Been There Now Helps Others," *YM*, June–July 2001.

Bob Levin, "The Kids Who Make It in from the Cold," *Maclean's*, December 21, 1998.

Susan Littwin, "Moving Up," *Rosie*, December 2001.

Warwick Mansell, "Bullies Drive Children to Run Away," *Times Educational Supplement*, November 12, 1999.

Ruby J. Martinez, "Understanding Runaway Teens," *Journal of Child and Adolescent Psychiatric Nursing*, May 2006.

Elizabeth Murray, "Liz's Story," *New York Times Upfront*, January 31, 2000.

Emily Nussbaum, "His Only Address Was an E-Mail Account," *New York Times Magazine*, September 17, 2000.

Helaine Olen, "Taking It to the Streets," *Salon.com*, February 12, 2007.

Tod Olson, "Where the Sidewalk Ends," *Teen People*, October 1999.

Marsha Recknagel, "Halfway Home," *Vogue*, September 2001.

Carla Rivera, "Evicting the Homeless Youths of Hollywood," *Los Angeles Times*, March 2, 2001.

Suzanne Smalley and Seth Mnookin, "A House of Horrors: In New York, Runaways Tell Story of Nightmarish Abuse." *Newsweek*, May 5, 2003.

Rachel Louise Synder, "Gimme Shelter," *Seventeen*, October 2000.

Nona Willis-Aronowitz, "It's a Trans World," *Salon.com*, January 5, 2007.

Index